101 Business Letters

Save hours writing letters

How long does a business letter take you to compose? 20 minutes? 30 minutes? An hour? In a year, that adds up to a colossal amount of time. Just think of the benefits that saving just a few minutes per letter could bring you. During a year it could amount to many, many hours of your time.

All the letters in this book may be copied straight from the page, and some will require only a slight amendment. With other letters, you may want to take a phrase here or a paragraph there and slot it into the rest of your letter. The important thing to remember is that the 'thinking' has already been done for you - so, those difficult situations, where you can't quite get the right words together, can now be banished ... forever.

Do you realise what it's costing you to write a letter?

Each letter that you write could be costing your business as much as £15 or more to send out, once your 'thinking' time (and overheads) have been taken into account. With over 100 letters in this guide (each costing a fraction of this amount), think how many pounds you will save by slicing hours off your letter-writing time.

Incisive commentaries

Identifying how subtle tones in a letter are achieved using different phrases is not always easy to pinpoint. What makes, for example, the tone in a letter of complaint either friendly, neutral, angry, diplomatic or strong? To help you find the answer, each letter in this book comes with its own incisive commentary, many of which highlight the specific words and phrases that alter the tone. The commentaries also clarify the meaning that is implicit in the words chosen, and demonstrate how a recipient will perceive and interpret those phrases, helping you to get exactly what you want.

Finding the letter you want is easy

The guide has an utterly comprehensive Contents page, which groups the letters by topic (*Suppliers, Customers, Debt collection* etc.). Each topic is then subdivided into further categories, for example, under *Suppliers* you will find (amongst others) *Making complaints - friendly and firm approaches* and *Making complaints - using a stronger tone*. Each letter is also numbered for ease of reference.

But what if you want to look up all the letters concerned with say, negotiating? All you have to do is turn to the *Index of letters by type* on page xiii, where a comprehensive list of these letters (and other types) will be found. For a final catch-all, there is a comprehensive topic index at the end of the work.

iii

Copyright

No matter what letter you have to write, *101 Business Letters* offers countless ways of phrasing business letters. Use it regularly and it will amply repay you, not only in time saved, but also in helping you to clinch deals, get debts paid quickly, obtain better prices and persuade people to your way of thinking. Whatever the letter, I wish you every success.

Two value-packed books

There were so many letters we wanted to include that there simply wasn't the space within one volume. So, a companion book, *101 more Business Letters* has been created giving you even more letters to choose from. While the overall subject areas are similar, you will find that the letters, their situations and the lessons to be learned are all different. Here are just some of the letters and topics to be found in *101 more Business Letters*:

- Dealing with non-delivery of goods
- Playing one client off against each other
- Handling a very rude customer
- Surveying customer attitudes
- Rejecting a speculative job application
- Announcing a credit surcharge on all accounts
- Making an offer of employment
- Announcing a bonus
- Summary dismissal
- Motivating an employee whose performance has deteriorated
- Offering condolences
- Managing public relations
- Keeping the bank informed about positive and deteriorating situations

While all the *letters* in each volume are different, we have kept the appendixes and introduction to each volume the same. The appendixes will probably be one of the most sought after sections (by your colleagues as well as yourself) and we feel it is important to make this information accessible in each volume. So, if a colleague happens to 'borrow' one of the volumes, you won't be left high and dry! Unless, of course, *both* volumes have been 'borrowed', in which case I recommend you buy another set!

David Crosby
January 1997

CONTENTS

CHAPTER 1 **Managing Suppliers**

CHAPTER 2 Managing Customers

CHAPTER 3 Debt Collection and Credit Control

CHAPTER 4 Employing People

CHAPTER 5   Sales and Marketing Management

CHAPTER 6   Banking, Insurance and Property

CHAPTER 7   International Trade

CHAPTER 8   Business and the Community

Acknowledgements

The Publisher would like to thank the customers who contributed letters to this guide, including: David Lambert of APTECH, DR Radia of NRG Victory Reinsurance Ltd, and Martin Oates of BSG Products. Special thanks also to Vic Blake of Cambridge for his contributions to the work.

INDEX OF LETTERS BY TYPE

This index is designed to be used with the contents and the main index at the end of the work. The Contents gives a good overview of the letters concerned with suppliers, customers, employees and so on. But, if you have to write a requesting letter (and want to compare these kinds of letters that are spread throughout the work), it is difficult to find them easily by examining the Contents. However, if you look up *Requesting* in this index you will find a list of the letters featured, that are concerned with this topic.

Apologising

Appealing

Appreciating

Asking (see also Requesting)

Cancelling

Complaining

Confirming

Correcting

Declining

Warning

Welcoming

CHAPTER ONE

Managing Suppliers

Suppliers often need to be held on a tight rein. Whether you need to query a quotation, place an order, negotiate a special arrangement, or simply want to make a complaint using a stern reproach, this chapter offers ideas and solutions designed to keep your suppliers firmly under your control. Just a few of the highlights are featured here.

Need to negotiate a rate with a supplier?
Suppliers may suggest a rate that is not feasible. Letter 11 shows how to clinch a deal without over-stretching your budget.

Do you need to fire a strong warning shot at a supplier?
It is a common trick for a supplier to agree a competitive price but then for that price to creep up over a period. Letter 12 shows how to adopt a polite but firm stance that demonstrates to your supplier just how far you are prepared to go.

Don't shy away from changing your terms and conditions
If things are not going the way you want them to, you may have to change the terms and conditions with a supplier. Don't shy away from it just because other terms were agreed previously. Letter 10 shows how to present new terms to a supplier so that they are readily accepted and there is no quibble about them.

Making a stern reproach
When complaining, make sure that you strike the right note to produce the desired response. Too harsh, and you risk alienating your suppliers. Too soft, and they may walk all over you. Six different letters portray some of the options available to you.

This is a standard request for a quotation. It is brief and to the point and the formality is appropriate for a new supplier. Note the specification of part numbers accompanying each item. This avoids any ambiguity about what items are to be supplied, particularly with the steel brackets, of which there are two different types.

Fenner & Sons

16 George Street, Woodbridge,
Suffolk IP3 7KL
Tel: (01394) 198423
Fax: (01394) 198444
Registered in England: 91221299
VAT No: 919129075 80

Mr J M Hibberd
Sales Manager
Pecklacks (Metals) Ltd
Drovers Lane
Slough
SL42 3RG

31 May 1999

Dear Mr Hibberd

Please supply a quotation for the following:

Item:	Part No:	Unit:	Quantity:
1.5″ Aluminium Trunking	B14375	3 metre	10
Lock Nuts	J388851	each	60
2″ Mild Steel Bolts	J388232	each	60
Closing Strip	B13650	3 metre	10
Steel Brackets	C18724	each	27
Steel Brackets	C18725	each	3

Delivery will be to Cardiff and we are looking for a delivery date within ten days of placing our order.

We would appreciate your quotation by fax and at the latest by Thursday 12 June.

Yours sincerely

Patrick Thompson
Production Manager

Hart & Tucker Ltd
19 Green Street, Maidstone, Kent ME41 1TJ
Telephone: (01622) 109109
Facsimile: (01622) 108106
Reg. No: England 96223978 VAT No: 91210674

Ms Sally Patterson
Sales Manager
Colourfast Printing
245 Downfields Ind. Est.
Maidstone
Kent
ME3 3ED

23 May 1999

Dear Ms Patterson

Your quotation: SL 3490
Thanks for your quotation for printing 2000 booklets.

I have just one query. The price.

As you know, I used to deal with your Halstead branch prior to our relocation last month. Three months ago, we placed an identical order for a related project. The extent is the same, the paper quality is the same and the quantity is the same. So why is your price 25% higher?

Yours sincerely

Jean Oilson
Production Manager

Price is often a sensitive issue between suppliers and customers. Here, a customer clearly senses that she is not being treated as well as she was by another branch of the same printing firm.

It is important not to jump to immediate conclusions and accuse the supplier of foul play. There may, after all, be a perfectly valid excuse.

The style of the two short sentences in the second paragraph ("I have just one query. The price.") puts the reader on the spot but stops short of making an accusation.

This is a simple letter to accompany a purchase order for a supplier with whom a credit account has not been opened.

Sending a cheque with the order should result in prompt service. Although the delivery details and date by when the goods are required should already be on the purchase order, it does no harm to spell them out in a letter as well. It also gives you the opportunity to confirm special instructions, as with the packing specifications here.

⊛ **WILSON SMITH LTD**

A wholly-owned subsidiary of The Wilson Group PLC
16 Willow Walk, Retford, Nottingham NG6 8WS
Tel: (01777) 121211 Fax: (01777) 121233
Reg. No: England 1212298762

Mr H Johnson
Sales Executive
P & J Electrical
Nuffield Ind. Est.
Morton, Retford
Nottingham
NG23 5TG

12 September 1999

Dear Mr. Johnson,

OUR ORDER NO. 10743
Please find our cheque to the value of £1123.60 to cover our order no. 10743. We require delivery on or by Thursday, 21st October 1999. Please ensure the items are packed in double-walled boxes, shrunk-wrapped on pallets.

Delivery address:-

Howlett & Son Ltd
Burston Industrial Estate
16 Garrard Street
Greenwich
London SE14

Please advise us of the delivery date as soon as possible.

Many thanks for your co-operation.

Yours sincerely,

Penny Taylor
Buyer

Wright & Simpson

157 Colder Way
Basingstoke
Hants RG21 5TG
Tel: (01256) 125907
Fax: (01256) 190986

Mr J Matthews
Sales Manager
Bull (Prints) Limited
Tillman's Trading Estate
Bristol
BS21 2LG

23 June 1999

Dear Julian

Re: Our Order No. 11978
I am sorry if this messes you around but our client has just notified us
that they would like their order delivered into a different warehouse.
The goods should now be sent to:

Hobbles (Cambridge) Limited
Eagle Trading Estate
Colchester Road
Basildon
Essex
B4 9UO

I hope this doesn't cause you too much inconvenience.

Many thanks for your co-operation.

Yours sincerely

Edward Wright

Partners: EG Wright MA & FA Simpson

However much you plan, last-minute changes will often occur. A supplier may have already booked a carrier to deliver goods to one place and then someone else decides they should go to a different location. The opening in this letter helps to defuse any irritation that a supplier may feel, especially when he realises that the change is due to circumstances beyond your control.

The tone of this curt letter is designed to bring the supplier sharply into line. You need to be a little careful to ensure you are not over-reacting to the situation. It would be appropriate for a supplier who had ignored similar requests in the past.

The last comment "I look forward to continuing our business relationship on a more organised note" is in danger of putting the reader's back up as it sounds like a personal attack – even if it is not intended that way. It could be rephrased as 'I trust our purchase order instructions will be rigidly adhered to in future', which apportions no blame but gets the same message across.

RPP Holdings Plc
35/38 New Road, Paignton, Devon TQ3 4UU
Tel: 01803 175653 Fax: 01803 187908
Reg. No: England 1976143

Mr J Patel
Sales Co-ordinator
Charles Bright Limited
63 Crow Lane
Brentwood
Essex
CM15 2AM

28 September 1999

Dear Mr Patel,

Our purchase order no. R467985
Thank you for your latest delivery, received today.

I would like to draw to your attention a very important point, which has been missed with the processing of this order.

On the purchase order, it is stated that your delivery note must be marked for the attention of Thomas Jones and, more importantly, contain our purchase order number. This is vital to us when we are receiving hundreds of items a day.

As this is a new request from us, we shall not be delaying payment as stated on the order but please bear this arrangement in mind for future business.

I hope you will appreciate the necessity behind this instruction and I look forward to continuing our business relationship on a more organised note.

Yours sincerely

Nina Lynch
Purchasing Manager

B & R HENDERSONS LTD
Marlows Road, Aberdeen AB20 5GT
Tel: 01224 267855 Fax: 01224 267977
Reg. No: 16497811 VAT No: 7387945

Frank O'Neil
Marketing Manager
Benton Copleys
Roundtree House
Kennet
Newmarket
CB8 7LP

25 April 1999

Dear Frank,

Your invoice no. 143880
I have received your statement requesting payment of invoice no. 143880
for £156.77, dated 30 July.

I understand that the items received against this invoice were sent in
error and the goods ordered are out of stock at your warehouse.

Please could you arrange for a credit note to be issued for the full
amount of £156.77. We shall be settling the remaining invoices at the
end of this month.

Yours sincerely

David Barker
Purchasing Manager

Someone has processed an order incorrectly and the wrong goods have been sent. A common enough mistake. This letter explains to the person in accounts exactly what the position is and why payment is not being made against the invoice. It ends on a reassuring note, saying to them when payment for other outstanding items will be made.

Carriage charges are often a source of contention. Companies supplying goods are aware that it costs a lot of money to deliver them. Equally, the business placing the order wants to keep the price as low as possible.

Some invoices may carry a carriage charge, added automatically when they are produced. This could explain how this 'error' occurred – or it could be a case of the supplier trying it on. Either way, a short letter, backed up with the knowledge that you had specified carriage be included in the quote, should put matters straight. "I was surprised ..." sets a gentle but firm tone for the reader.

Thomas King & Palmer Ltd
serving the world

24 Fuller Road, Welling,
Kent DA16 7JP
Tel : (01322) 100132
Fax : (01322) 100178

Reg. No : England 1212298762
VAT No : 92905643

Henry Fuller
Sales Manager
Savill Plastics Ltd
Saxon Way
Hitchin
Herts
HN7 5TG

23 June 1999

Dear Henry,

Your invoice no. 29783
Thank you for your invoice no. 29783 for £7800.

I was surprised to see a carriage charge included for £69. Your original quotation (no. LM89753) made no mention of an additional charge for delivery. As our purchase order specified that the goods be delivered carriage paid I was led to believe that this was included in your quotation.

Please could you send us a credit note for the full amount of the carriage.

Yours sincerely

Alan Scott
Purchasing Manager

Grange & Turner Ltd

32 WESTBOURN ROAD, WITNEY, OXON OX6 7HY

Telephone (01993) 107888
Fax (01993) 107843

Reg. No: England 13078453
VAT No: 75698764

Mr Tom Patterson
Managing Partner
T P Consultancy
234 Slade Street
Milton Keynes
MK43 7PL

7 August 1999

Dear Mr Patterson,

We are a small company specialising in business-to-business direct marketing. We are coming under increasing pressure from our clients to implement the BS EN ISO 9000 specification. We would therefore be interested to find out exactly what this would involve, in terms of man hours, cost and procedures.

Your name was passed to me by the Association of Quality Management Consultants as someone who is registered to advise in this area. I would be most grateful if you would agree to visit us and give us an introduction to the requirements, which I understand would be free of charge.

If you are available, please would you ring me at the above number to fix a mutually convenient time.

Thank you for your kind attention. I look forward to hearing from you.

Yours sincerely

William Barker
Marketing Director

Not everything can be bought off the shelf by simply quoting a product name and price. With professional services, there will be a process of exploring what is required before agreeing terms. This letter seeks a consultant to help implement the ISO 9000 standard.

The writer could have given more details about the size of the company – how many employees there are, size of turnover, breakdown of the activities and so on. But equally, these will occur in the course of the subsequent telephone conversation. It may even be preferable to arouse the reader's curiosity – a useful tactic to ensure a swift response.

It is always useful to say how you got hold of their name. If it was a referral and you are competing for attention, naming your common source can help to build a rapport. Note the close. Thanking the recipient before he has even responded is a convenient way of putting an obligation on him to reply.

Delivery instructions often need to be given after an order has been placed. If more than one order from your company is going through the supplier at any one time, you need to make sure the original purchase order number is given, to avoid confusion.

Delivery instructions should also give a contact name and be marked for the attention of a named person. It can be all too easy for goods to be delivered to a company and for the person who placed the order to be the last to find out, because none of the accompanying documentation gives his or her name.

RPP Holdings Plc
35/38 New Road, Paignton, Devon TQ3 4UU
Tel: 01803 175653 Fax: 01803 187908
Reg. No: England 1976143

Jane Summers
Marketing Executive
Corrugated Card & Packaging Ltd
Unit 8 London Road Ind. Est.
Truro
Cornwall
TR9 7KM

27 July 1999

Dear Jane,

Purchase order number 548792
Please arrange for the consignment of 500 cardboard boxes to be delivered to our Middleton warehouse. The address is:

Unit 4
The Middleton Business Park
Angles Lane
Middleton
MD3 4XZ

The consignment should be marked for the attention of Mr Jeff Holmes, our Warehouse Manager.

Yours sincerely

Helen Meeting
Supplies Manager

Grange & Turner Ltd

32 WESTBOURN ROAD, WITNEY, OXON OX6 7HY

Telephone (01993) 107888
Fax (01993) 107843

Reg. No: England 13078453
VAT No: 75698764

Terry Coles
Sales Manager
C & D Print Services
33 Top Street
Aldermaston
Reading
RG7 8JU

22 November 1999

Dear Terry

Re: Deliveries

As you know, we deal with a number of different printers and print suppliers. Over the last year or so <u>all</u> have had at least one problem, due to insufficiently labelled deliveries.

We have tried to suggest systems to help both printer and supplier to prevent this problem, but on the whole, we have been politely ignored (or conveniently forgotten), once the immediate problem is over.

So we now feel that we have to insist that a good system for recording deliveries is adhered to by both suppliers and printers and below is what we propose.

All boxes of printed matter should in future be labelled as follows:

1. Sample of the contents on top of the box
2. On the side of the box:
   - Quantity of items in the box
   - Scratch code of the item
   - Promotion code
   There should be no other codes, which may cause confusion on the boxes.
3. On the dispatch note: total quantity of each item, by scratch code.

Our suppliers to whom you send items will be required to count in the boxes and confirm that the quantity supplied matches the dispatch note, and that there are sufficient boxes as indicated by the Job Sheet supplied by us. They will also be required to fax us a confirmation of the quantity received and any shortfall. This will also ensure that any problems are noted in good time, to prevent delivery being delayed.

We would be very grateful for your co-operation in this, which is designed to protect all of us. To assist with its compliance, we will be adding a penalty clause, with immediate effect, that a failure to label the boxes and count them in to the mailing house correctly will result in delay of payment of 30 days <u>beyond</u> our normal credit terms with you.

Thank you for your assistance in this matter.

Yours sincerely

Helen Mace
Production Manager

You may at some time need to revise your systems if you find that they are not working well. Note how the suggestion here starts off relatively softly "...this is what we propose..." and "...we would be very grateful for your co-operation...", aiming to win the supplier over.

However, the implementation of a 'stick' element in "...we will be adding a penalty clause..." noticeably gives the supplier no choice, even though the first part sounds as if the supplier has a say in the matter. This is confirmed by the closing line, which doesn't ask for their reaction but simply presents it as a *fait accompli*.

If a supplier suggests a rate for a job that is not feasible it may be better to go back to them with a fixed figure that you are prepared to spend and see if an agreement can be reached.

The friendly tone will reassure the supplier that the intention is sincere and it is not simply a question of trying to tie him down on price. The rhetorical question at the end "Are you game?" acts as a challenge and is designed to clinch the deal.

Thomas King & Palmer Ltd

serving the world

24 Fuller Road, Welling,
Kent DA16 7JP
Tel : (01322) 100132
Fax : (01322) 100178

Reg. No : England 1212298762
VAT No : 92905643

Mr D R West
67 Millers Lane
Tackley
Oxford
OX6 3AG

26 May 1999

Dear David,

Corporate newsletter
Thanks for your fax of 9th May. Sorry that I have sat on it for so long – particularly as my need is so urgent!!

While a daily charge sounds logical, I am uncomfortable with it because neither of us knows how long these things are going to take to produce. And anyway, some will take longer than others, depending on the available resources.

So, I have an alternative suggestion to make which, I think, is fair.

We put £350 *per newsletter* on the table to write it. So, following a thorough discussion and briefing, you do what you feel is reasonable for that amount of money. The intention is not to squeeze a quart out of a pint pot. It is to see what we can achieve within that sort of budget. Are you game?

I look forward to hearing from you.

Kind regards

Yours sincerely

Kay Mitchell
Marketing Manager

Hart & Tucker Ltd

19 Green Street, Maidstone, Kent ME41 1TJ
Telephone: (01622) 109109
Facsimile: (01622) 108106
Reg. No: England 96223978   VAT No: 91210674

Terry Coles
Sales Manager
C & D Print Services
33 Top Street
Aldermaston
Reading
RG7 8JU

22 September 1999

Dear Terry

Re: Your charges
Thank you for your letter of 12th September and for taking the trouble to clarify the situation for me. I am sorry that I had to ask you to do this because our files had got into such a mess.

I can see that I must accept the invoices raised on promotions 102 and 109 as having been agreed. However, I believe that Claire is still waiting for a breakdown of your invoice for order 118. We are not satisfied that there was £300 of origination work required when we sent you all new film and we are also disputing the charge for the amendments.

Next year
The unfortunate fact of the matter is that with these carriage and origination charges, as well as the higher base price of £1100, it has cost us up to £400 a month *more* to put work through you rather than through our other printers. And we have no control over the variables - we don't know whether carriage is going to be £200 or £500 for the year. We don't know whether the proofs are going to be £90 or £500 a time.

There is no question about the quality of your work. It is comparable with the quality we receive from our other suppliers. But the price you charge for our jobs is simply too high.

I am afraid that, unless you can find a way to do our printing profitably for a flat rate of £1100, we will probably have to agree to part company.

Yours sincerely

Tony Green
Marketing Director

This letter is designed to send a strong message. It tries to make the supplier face up to the reality of the situation.

It starts off gently but firmly: "The unfortunate fact of the matter...". Note how the additional expense is very slightly exaggerated (or made to appear more serious) by adding the words "...up to £400...", £400 being the worst case, not the average case.

A polite but firm stance is maintained to the end "...we will probably have to agree to part company...", the 'probably' leaving the door open for further negotiations but signalling at the same time how far you are prepared to go.

When the wrong goods are sent, you want the error to be corrected quickly. Here someone has inverted the numbers 60 and 30 for the quantity and size. A simple request to have them changed should be sufficient. The invoice will have mentioned the correct quantity and size, so this doesn't need to be changed. It should, however, be referred to in the letter, so the company can identify it on its system easily. Note how the writer tries to avoid the confusion by putting the quantity (sixty) in words and the size (30) in numbers.

If you do return goods to a company, always send them separately from a letter asking for replacements. Returns often get put to one side to be dealt with later – sometimes weeks later. It could be disastrous if your letter requesting corrective action is held up amongst the returns.

IDENDEN INDUSTRIES
A division of Idenden Plc
Porter House, Hull HU7 4RF England

Tel 01482 119087 Fax 01482 119088
Registered in England No: 1218943

Ms Elizabeth Taylor
Sales Co-ordinator
Litson & Fulton Ltd
Unit 8 Clifton Ind. Est.
Clifton Road
Liverpool
L9 6DD

24 October 1999

Dear Elizabeth,

Our purchase order no. YTL8906
Yesterday, we received sixty 30mm clips for high velocity piping, which were supplied against your invoice no LP1018 dated 20 October.

Our purchase order no. YTL8906 clearly asked for thirty 60 mm clips. I would be grateful if you could supply the correct items to us by return.

The 30mm clips are being returned to you under separate cover.

Yours sincerely

Stuart O'Neil
Purchasing Manager

RPP Holdings Plc
35/38 New Road, Paignton, Devon TQ3 4UU
Tel: 01803 175653 Fax: 01803 187908
Reg. No: England 1976143

Jane Summers
Marketing Executive
Corrugated Card & Packaging Ltd
Unit 8
London Road Ind. Est.
Truro
Cornwall
TR9 7KM

1 October 1999

Dear Jane

Purchase order number 548792

Thanks for your delivery of cardboard boxes received yesterday.

Once again, gremlins appear to have intervened and kidnapped 49 cardboard boxes out of the consignment. We are waiting for the ransom demand. Or perhaps they were hijacked by homeless people looking for a new cardboard duvet for the night?

Please, please, please supply us with the missing items ASAP.

Yours sincerely

Helen Meeting
Office Manager

This fairly unconventional letter should be reserved for people with whom you have built up a good relationship and have a clear understanding.

A jokey response like this (particularly when it is in a complaint setting) should score you many points with your supplier. Its aim is to evoke a positive reaction in the reader so that they feel more inclined to respond favourably to your request. Its danger, which you should be aware of, is that your supplier takes you for granted and thinks that, because you are taking a light-hearted approach, you are prepared to put up with the poor service.

Note how a more casual tone is created by using abbreviated phrases and terms: "Thanks for" instead of the more formal "Thank you for" and "ASAP" in place of "as soon as possible".

The aim of this letter is to fire a warning shot at the supplier and shake him into changing his attitude towards you.

Clearly, the supplier has taken your company's business for granted for too long. The poor performance is made to sound worse when contrasted against the "impeccable" service that you received at the outset. The catalogue of general mistakes is then supported by a specific incident that has finally broken your faith in the supplier.

If the supplier has the will, he will make the changes, but if he doesn't make amends then the customer leaves no doubt that the business will go elsewhere: "We shall have no option ..." emphasises how far you are prepared to go. It is a useful phrase that is very handy in negotiations. Beware of using it lightly though: if you say it, make sure you are prepared to carry it out.

B & R HENDERSONS LTD
Marlows Road, Aberdeen AB20 5GT
Tel: 01224 267855 Fax: 01224 267977
Reg. No: 16497811 VAT No: 7387945

Mr Andrew McBride
Manager
Scottish Stationery Supplies
45 High Road
Aberdeen
AB19 2EW

26 July 1999

Dear Andrew,

I am writing to express my growing dissatisfaction with the service we are receiving from Scottish Stationery Supplies.

For the first year, the service you gave us was impeccable. Since then, though, we have noticed a gradual deterioration. The goods are frequently out of stock or taking longer for you to supply; you do not respond to our requests as speedily as before and the number of incorrect items delivered has increased. This was compounded this morning when, for the second time in a row, you supplied us with 5 boxes of C5 instead of C6 envelopes.

It is essential that all our suppliers give us the best possible service. We shall be monitoring the situation closely over the coming weeks, but if a significant improvement is not noticeable we shall have no option but to seek an alternative supplier.

Yours sincerely

Tina Vail
Office Manager

SIMPSON & MARTIN

39 TOP STREET
STOKE-ON-TRENT
ST2 3DR UNITED KINGDOM
Tel: (01782) 156232 Fax: (01782) 120899

Reg. No: England 96223978 VAT No: 91210674

Mr R Henderson
JKB Builders
16 Ponts Hill
Wysall
Stoke-on-Trent
ST4 5HT

23 September 1999

Dear Mr Henderson,

39 Top Street, Stoke-on-Trent

A week ago you arranged for a 3-foot high boundary wall to be repaired outside our property.

The work was completed to our specification, but this morning it was noticed that the mortar used to bind the bricks together has cracked, to such an extent that it is not only flaking away but several of the bricks are now in danger of becoming loose.

Would you kindly arrange for someone to come and remedy the defective work as soon as possible?

Yours sincerely

John Good
Managing Director

When asking for repairs to be done, you need to emphasise how serious the situation is. Here, the work seemed satisfactory when it was done but within a short period it is clear that all is not well.

This letter leaves the request to put it right until the end. Blame is not apportioned directly (it could be the fault of the type of cement used) but note the use of the phrase "...come and remedy the defective work...", which implies heavily that the supplier is being held responsible.

If a supplier suddenly goes very quiet following a complaint you need to try to open the channels of communication again.

Although it will be irritating to you, and you may be feeling very annoyed, your letter should retain a tone of calm professionalism. There will be plenty of time to vent your feelings later. Your goal now is to force the supplier to respond. Reminding him that you are withholding payment should be sufficient to make him react.

SIMPSON & MARTIN

39 TOP STREET
STOKE-ON-TRENT
ST2 3DR UNITED KINGDOM
Tel: (01782) 156232 Fax: (01782) 120899
Reg. No: England 96223978 VAT No: 91210674

Mr F Benson
Benson Envelopes
Unit 5 Longacre Ind. Est.
Stoke-on-Trent
ST5 7VB

30 August 1999

Dear Mr Benson

Our purchase order no. AB54673
I am extremely disappointed that I find myself having to write to you yet again.

I wrote to you on 9 August concerning a consignment of 50,000 C5 envelopes (printed one colour on front only) which we received from you on 6 August. A copy of my letter is enclosed. I remind you that we are withholding payment as the goods are defective.

Since then, a week has passed and I have received no reply from you, nor the replacement envelopes. I have telephoned several times but my calls have not been returned.

Please telephone me on receipt of this letter, to let me know when we can expect to receive the replacement order.

Yours sincerely

Vera Young
Marketing Production Manager

Kelso Limited

16 Abbots Road, Luton, Bedford MK44 7YT
Tel: (01234) 136953 Fax: (01234) 136422
Registered in England No: 9126719 VAT No: 91523489 76

Mr Hardy
Sales Manager
Cambridge Cutters Ltd
Gratton Road
Cambridge
CB1 1MJ

2 December 1999

Dear Mr Hardy

Our order no. 64987

I was given your verbal assurance on Tuesday that you would have
no problem in completing the cutting processes requested for the
folder order placed with you last week and delivering them to us on
the Wednesday, in time for us to complete our processes. The
order was booked in well in advance and we delivered the items to
you at the time agreed.

I was therefore astounded to find that not only had you not
completed the processes and returned the order to us by yesterday,
but that we were not kept informed why the order would not be
completed on time.

As your failure to comply with our terms will mean that our client will
seek compensation from us for untimely delivery, we shall deduct
any losses that we incur from your invoice.

Yours sincerely

John Piggott
Sales Director

A verbal assurance is still a contract and one that here has been broken. The letter veers towards an angry tone when it uses the phrase "I was astounded..." but elsewhere retains its sense of measured annoyance.

Good phrases to remember to use when an agreement has been breached is the one: "...failure to comply with our terms..." and "...seeking recompense for any losses that we incur." It should be sufficient to put the wind up them.

Occasionally, a supplier will not play ball and may attempt to put up a fight. He may have decided (for whatever reason) that your business is not worth retaining.

Matters here are coming to a head. The supplying company is attempting to wriggle out of the complaint, but the customer is having none of it and knows that the law is on its side.

The phrase "we have now decided to take legal advice...with a view to recovery of our money..." and "...instructions will be issued to our solicitors to proceed against you" are designed to leave the supplier in no doubt that he must pay up or face legal action.

GKT Products Ltd, Unit 10, Castleway Lane, Alloway, Ayr, KA7 4BE
Telephone (01292) 177900 Fax (01292) 199855   Reg. No: 17964583 VAT No: 679845

Mr Paul Newman
Marketing Executive
Computer & Stationery Supplies
Parkside Business Park
Oakham
Leicester
LE4 7HJ

28 April 1999

Dear Mr Newman

Our order 219784
I refer to your letter of 23rd April 1999 about a consignment of faulty computer disks that we received from you on April 5th.

In your letter you claim that these disks are of the highest quality and would, therefore, have left your premises in perfect condition. You presume, therefore, that they must have been mishandled in some way by us and that the fault is, therefore, ours. You also state that these disks were supplied at a special promotional discount and that discounted goods are not subject to replacement or refund. This point, you maintain, would have been made clear to us at the time of purchase.

I must point out to you that we have many years experience and our staff are highly trained and know very well how to handle and store computer disks. We can assure you that these disks **were** faulty at the time we received them. We do not doubt your company's ability to handle such equipment but feel particularly aggrieved that you feel free to doubt ours. On this point alone, we have decided to have no more dealings with your company.

On the matter of the special promotional discount, you can be assured that at no time was any caveat given to us regarding refunds. You will also be aware that the Sale of Goods Act 1979 states quite clearly that faulty goods **are** subject to refund or replacement. A simple disclaimer on your part does not alter the law in any way.

We have now decided to take legal advice on this matter, with a view to recovery of our money and you are advised that, unless a full refund is received from you within three days, instructions will be issued to our solicitors to proceed against you.

As stated, we will be having no further dealings with your company.

Yours sincerely,

Betty Davis
Purchasing Manager

CHAPTER TWO

Managing Customers

The Customer is King. But knowing that doesn't make it any easier when you have an awkward one to manage, or mistakes happen that need to be sorted. There can be few matters less pleasant than an irate customer, and few more gratifying than one who is satisfied. The letters in this chapter provide a wealth of ideas for keeping relations with customers on an even keel and, when the waters turn choppy, what you can do to calm them down again.

Saying sorry

It sounds simple, but how many customers genuinely believe what you say? Saying sorry sincerely, so that a customer decides to stay with you rather than move to your competition, is an art. Letter 28 is an example of one that genuinely worked.

What if they are trying it on?

Sometimes, you may find yourself up against a customer who is being economical with the truth. You can't openly accuse them of lying, so how do you handle it? Letter 29 shows how.

The easiest source of new business?

Your existing customers are your easiest source of new business. They have used you once and, if they enjoyed the experience, they will come back to you again, and again. Taking the time and trouble to thank them may not seem a profitable use of your time but it will reap rewards. Letters 33–35 give plenty of ideas.

Don't forget your lapsed customers

These ones are well worth trying to revive. You won't get them all back, but just a few will make the effort worthwhile. See letter 37.

This quotation is to a customer who the supplier already knows. It doesn't have the formality of a quotation form. The supplier knows that the customer probably doesn't wants more than 100kg and so doesn't bother to provide the figures, but leaves the option open. He also ends the letter confidently, expecting the order.

Note how the supplier is using his skill to advise the customer on what he believes will be the best option, given the specification that has been asked for. This kind of service will be appreciated, and the customer may be more inclined to place an order, because he knows his requirements will be looked after.

If the customer had to choose between one supplier who offered a straight quote and this supplier who is offering a quote and helpful advice, it is easy to see which one he is likely to opt for.

⊛ WILSON SMITH LTD

A wholly-owned subsidiary of The Wilson Group PLC
16 Willow Walk, Retford, Nottingham NG6 8WS
Tel: (01777) 121211 Fax: (01777) 121233
Reg. No: England 1212298762

Mr G Benn
Sales Manager
Drake & Huggins Ltd
Orchard Road
Saffron Walden
Essex
CB21 6HN

19 August 1999

Dear Gordon,

I confirm our faxed quotation for yellow ruling powder at £6.00 per kg. If you require more than 100kg, we can offer you better prices.

I enclose the standard colour range. Please note that, although, we are able to produce a lemon yellow, this appears rather dull. I have therefore excluded it, as I believe your client specified it should be bright. Also, the royal blue and black print up much more strongly than in the sample shown, as these prints have been produced on the wrong paper. I am getting some more drawn up on the correct substrate and will forward them to you as soon as they are available.

I look forward to hearing from you and, of course, to receiving your order.

Yours sincerely,

John Wilson
Sales Director

H J KINGSLEY (NORWICH) LTD

Kingsley House, Morris Street, Norwich NR6 7JM
Tel: (01603) 117097 Fax: (01603) 117099 Reg. No: England 12086215 VAT No: 8793519

Mr W Johns
General Manager
Gurteen & Parker
Unit 7 Meadowview Ind. Est.
Norwich
NR2 4ED

15 February 1999

Dear Mr Johns

Nobo 90 Overhead Projector
Thank you for your letter querying the price of the Nobo 90 Overhead
Projector.

I confirm the price of this item is £595 (excluding VAT) and not £409
as previously stated. It seems that the person who took your original
call misheard the model number. I apologise for this error. However, as
I am sure you have already discovered, the Nobo 99 has the advantages
of being both more compact and lighter than the Nobo 90, as well as
having better-quality lenses. All Nobo models come with a 12-month,
on-site guarantee.

I am sorry if this oversight has caused you any inconvenience. As a
token of our appreciation of your custom, we are pleased to offer you a
free telescopic pointer with your order.

Yours sincerely

Marilyn Morris
Sales Director

A supplier here has misquoted a price. It may be that the customer thought he was going to be getting a bargain of a better model at a lower price. The customer's reaction is bound to be one of disappointment, especially as he is being asked to pay almost another £200.

The supplier, concerned that this may be enough to deter the customer, works hard to retain the business by taking the opportunity of pointing out the additional features of the more expensive model.

To draw the sting of the higher price the supplier offers a nice surprise to the customer – a small free item, which will go a long way towards retaining the goodwill of the customer, which will far outweigh the cost of the pointer.

Taking the trouble to welcome a new customer is a good opportunity to offer thanks for their custom.

Here, the business has to get the customer to sign an agreement – potentially tricky, as it is an opportunity for the customer to decide they don't want your service after all.

Instead of stressing that the customer is now committing herself to the agreement, the writer cunningly puts himself into the shoes of the customer, when he says these are "...our promises 'and your rights'..." a careful choice of phrase, designed to make the customer feel like a winner.

Note also how the process is made to seem so easy "...simply sign both copies...".

IDENDEN INDUSTRIES
A division of Idenden Plc
Porter House, Hull HU7 4RF England

Tel 01482 119087 Fax 01482 119088
Registered in England No: 1218943

Mrs J Holmes
Holmes and Barker Associates
23 Holly Bush Lane
Stretham
Cambs
CB8 4JK

16 August 1999

Dear Mrs Holmes

Your order no: BYR 99854WE
Thank you for your order.

We have arranged for an engineer to call at your premises to fit your boiler on the morning of the 6 September 1999, if this is convenient for you.

We note that you have opted for our full-service agreement to cover maintenance of the boiler and any spare parts. I enclose a service agreement, listing the conditions under which maintenance and parts will be supplied, together with a copy of our 12 months-guarantee, which sets out our promises (and your rights if we fail to live up to any of them).

Please check all the details. If you are happy with them, simply sign both copies of the agreement and return one to us in the return envelope provided.

If you have any queries, please do not hesitate to call us on 01482 119087, from 9am to 5pm, Monday to Saturday.

We look forward to welcoming you as a customer.

Yours sincerely

Robert Patterson
Account Manager

⊛ WILSON SMITH LTD

A wholly-owned subsidiary of The Wilson Group PLC
16 Willow Walk, Retford, Nottingham NG6 8WS
Tel: (01777) 121211 Fax: (01777) 121233
Reg. No: England 1212298762

Mr Winston Pathmanathan
Director
Kuantan Industries
5 Ipoh Street
5100 Kuala Lumpur
Malaysia

8 February 1999

Dear Winston,

Many thanks for your letter of 13th January.

Unfortunately, I think you have made a number of errors in your request, which has prevented me from sending you the pro forma invoices.

1. On all the plates you have requested 'Packets'. SORD, KORD AND ROLAND plates are packed 25 per packet and M1850 and G201 are 100 per packet. This would mean, for example, 1,250 KORD plates costing $6,787.50 and 5,000 1850 plates costing $7,250.00. If this is correct, your total consignment would cost about $65,000.

2. There are two sizes of ROLAND 3 plate, as specified in my letter of 15th October. Which size is required?

3. Do you require Negative or Positive plates for M1850 and GTO?

I would be grateful if you could answer these queries by return, so that we can process your order for you as soon as possible.

Yours sincerely,

James Smith
Marketing Director

Occasionally, customers may place an order but omit a fundamental piece of information or, as here, misunderstand how many items are in a packet. The more technical the item being requested, the more likely this is to occur.

Here, the supplier is asking the customer to confirm what is required. It can be dangerous to make assumptions about an order when it is not clear. The last thing this supplier would want to do is to send out the wrong items and find them coming flooding back, especially when the customer is being asked to pay in advance of receiving the items. Don't forget, even if the customer is in the wrong, it still puts you in a bad light.

A customer has made a mistake with an order and the supplier is responding. The supplier gives the buyer an option to amend part of the order as they are only part way through the job.

The supplier's reply is courteous and to the point. It could have taken a tougher line saying 'you *must* accept the 150 ringbinders already made'. Instead it takes the softer approach of "...we will have to ask you..." as he knows the customer is in the wrong and there is no need to add insult to injury.

RPP Holdings Plc
35/38 New Road, Paignton, Devon TQ3 4UU
Tel: 01803 175653 Fax: 01803 187908
Reg. No: England 1976143

FAX MESSAGE

To: Tom Greate
         Wilson Smith Ltd

Fax No: 01777 121233

From: Bob Taylor   Date: 22 February 1999

Dear Tom,

Your order no 30596
I received your fax this morning, requesting that your order for 500 ringbinders with a 30mm diameter ring be amended to binders that take 350 leaves.

Unfortunately, your order has already been in production for two days and we have made up 150 ringbinders. As these have been tailored to your requirements with your company's logo, we will have to ask you to accept the 150 ringbinders already made.

Please let me know today if you want a further 500 ringbinders with a 35mm diameter ring made or just 350.

Yours sincerely

Bob Taylor
Sales Manager

Grange & Turner Ltd

32 WESTBOURN ROAD, WITNEY, OXON OX6 7HY

Telephone (01993) 107888
Fax (01993) 107843

Reg. No: England 13078453
VAT No: 75698764

Mr P Brooks
33 Little Lane
East Bridgford
Nottingham
NG55 6YH

16 May 1999

Dear Mr Brooks

Thank you for taking the trouble to write, asking for your name to be removed from our mailing list. From today, your name and address will be excluded from all mailing lists produced here.

I should warn you that most mailings are prepared a long way in advance and it is almost certain that some are yet to be posted. I can only apologise for the irritation these further mailings may cause but please be assured that they will soon come to a stop.

However, if they cause you concern, and you would like me to carry out an additional check, simply return the unwanted letter using our FREEPOST address:

Jane Harvey
List Controller
Grange & Turner Ltd
FREEPOST
Witney
OX6 7HY

We are always keen to keep our mailing costs down, wherever possible, and to mail only those who wish to hear from us.

If you have any further questions please do not hesitate to contact me.

Yours sincerely

Jane Harvey
List Controller

Unwanted mail can be a major source of irritation – mainly to consumers. Businesses seem to accept more readily that it is part and parcel of their daily life. With most respectable companies, it should be possible to restrict the amount of direct mail you receive, simply by asking to be taken off their mailing lists.

This letter reassures the recipient that appropriate action is being taken. Note how it opens, thanking the customer for taking the trouble to write: a nice way of disarming a complainant.

The letter doesn't grovel but points out exactly what the person can expect to happen and it offers a course of action if things don't improve and reminds the consumer that it is in the company's interests, ultimately, to keep mailings down – something the person writing in would not think about automatically.

The company complaining about the poor service here believes that the cleaning company has ignored its first letter, even though it seems that it has genuinely gone astray. This is unfortunate, because it means the writer will have to work doubly hard to convince the customer that the fault is completely innocent. This is successfully achieved here.

Being seen to do more than is strictly required is a useful tactic for handling complaints. Here, the cleaning company takes the precaution of allocating a new person to the job and offering a discount off the month's invoice.

Be modest also in the extent to which you claim to be compensating the other party. Note how the writer says "...and trust that this *helps in* compensating for your dissatisfaction". He could have written "...and trust this compensates you for your dissatisfaction", which would appear slightly presumptuous and probably negate all the profuse apologies that have been made.

BAKER CLEANING SERVICES

29 Cunningham Street
London
N32 6JG
Telephone: (0171) 016 1350
Facsimile: (0171) 016 1351

Reg. No: England 118974165

Mrs E Bjornsen
General Manager
Hansoms Auctions
153 Simpson Street
London
WC3 4RT

10 July 1999

Dear Mrs Bjornsen,

Thank you for your letter of the 5th July, expressing concern over the cleaning service that we provide for your company.

You say that you have written to us once already on this matter but, having looked into this, we can find no record of ever having received your letter. We are not sure what happened here but we very much regret that this has meant a continuation of your problem.

In your letter, you state that toilet areas are not adequately cleaned or disinfected and that the office area, although always vacuumed properly, is often not dusted or polished.

I have spoken to the four staff who clean your offices on a rota and I believe I have now isolated the problem. Although the cause seems to have arisen out of a temporary problem affecting one of our cleaners, I have taken the precaution of assigning a permanent replacement to your team and I have reminded all cleaners that only the highest standards are acceptable.

I very much regret the inconvenience and disappointment caused and hope that the measures taken will now restore the service we offer to its former high standard. As a token of our goodwill, I have arranged for a discount of 30% off this month's invoice and trust that this helps in compensating for your dissatisfaction.

Once again, please accept our sincerest apologies.

Yours sincerely,

Jill Hooper
Account Manager

Taylor Taylor & Shaw

Benton House, Clifton, Bristol BS16 7LJ
Tel: (0117) 1089254   Fax: (0117) 1089211

Mr R Hodds
Director
RLO (of Bristol) Ltd
32 Gloucester Road
Clifton
Bristol
BS8 4UP

14 June 1999

Dear Bob

I am very sorry that you were left waiting at your offices for the meeting that we had arranged last week.

I know how frustrating it is to be left high and dry and I take all the blame for getting it wrong. I wrote your appointment down for 13 July instead of 13 June.

To make amends, can I offer you lunch when we meet? How are you fixed for 18 June at 12 o'clock? I suggest we meet at my office, if that is convenient to you.

Yours sincerely

Andrew W Taylor

PS I really do mean June this time!

Partners: AW Taylor & GS Taylor

The two people who were due to meet know each other well. Even though one of them has been inconvenienced, the tone is friendly, fitting their established relationship. Bob knows that Andrew Taylor is to be trusted and doesn't make a habit of missing appointments. If they had not known each other, a much more formal tone would be called for.

Even though the letter is friendly, note how the feeling is still sincere – Andrew empathises with Bob saying: "I know how frustrating it is to be left high and dry..." A recompense is offered in the form of a lunch. Another highlighting device is used with the PS – here Andrew wants to confirm that he really means June and has not made another mistake.

Letters that explain the reason for a mistake can give the customer an impression that you are being very defensive in passing the buck on to someone else instead of accepting responsibility for your actions. This can reduce still further the customer's estimation of you, rather than restoring his faith in your ability to deliver the services. This letter tackles this issue nicely in the second paragraph, with the phrase "If I could perhaps explain the circumstances, not as an excuse, but so you can see the exceptional...".

The sincerity of this letter is emphasised by the phrases "I was most disturbed..."; "...and I am deeply sorry..." and "This unfortunate event...". And it is not just simple apologies the reader is being asked to accept, but "unreserved" apologies. The use of these emphatic words builds up a greater sense of remorse.

RPP Holdings Plc
35/38 New Road, Paignton, Devon TQ3 4UU
Tel: 01803 175653 Fax: 01803 187908
Reg. No: England 1976143

Mr P Piggott
Managing Director
TMP UK Ltd
Manor Park
Hitchin
Herts
HP7 9UM

23 April 1999

Dear Mr Piggott

I was most disturbed to receive your letter of 20 April, informing me of your dissatisfaction with our performance. I am deeply sorry that we have let you and your client down. We take great care to ensure that our customers are satisfied, as this is essential to the continuation of our business.

If I could perhaps explain the circumstances, not as an excuse but so you can see the exceptional and unexpected difficulties we faced. When I telephoned you on Tuesday, your order was on track to be supplied the following day. Soon after we spoke, I had to leave the factory for an unavoidable meeting. An hour later, the machine developed a fault which took four hours to rectify and this meant we were unable to complete your order. Because I was expected back the same day, it was left for me to telephone you to explain the situation. By bad luck, I was detained longer than expected and did not return to the factory the same day.

This unfortunate event has highlighted a gap in our procedures, which we are correcting. In future, in my absence, our Production Manager will notify you of any deviation from the agreed schedule.

Please accept our unreserved apologies. We shall, subject to documentary proof, of course, make good any losses that you incur as a result of our failure to meet your deadline.

Yours sincerely

JH Hardy
Customer Services Manager

Grange & Turner Ltd

32 WESTBOURN ROAD, WITNEY, OXON OX6 7HY

Telephone (01993) 107888
Fax (01993) 107843

Reg. No: England 13078453
VAT No: 75698764

Mr T P Smith
124 Vale Road
Clifton
Bristol
BS5 7HY

24 July 1999

Dear Mr Smith,

Our Statement dated 12 April 1999
We have supplied you with books on four separate occasions to
the value of £75, for which we have asked for payment three
times.

You are claiming that you have never received the items ordered
and that they must have been lost in the post. Our carrier's
records demonstrate that the goods were despatched and each
time signed for by a D M Martin. You claim that no one of that
name lives at your address and that the goods must have been
incorrectly delivered.

We could understand if a parcel was incorrectly delivered on one
occasion but the fact that parcels have been delivered and
accepted four times by the same person seems very odd indeed.

As our debt cannot be settled and goods supplied to this address
are apparently not being received safely, we have no alternative
but to cease fulfilling orders to you. We shall write off the
amount of £75 on this occasion.

Yours sincerely

T P O'Neil
Customer Accounts Manager

Occasionally, you may come up against a situation where the facts just don't fit. You don't have the evidence to say: 'I don't believe you; you're lying', so how do you handle it? The simple business decision is to refuse to do business with the customer any more.

The supplier here produces the evidence that the goods are being delivered correctly and then in the third paragraph tells the customer that the supplier smells a rat with the phrases "...very odd indeed" and the fact that goods are "...apparently..." not being received safely. This gets as close to a specific challenge as you can afford.

The customer is the loser in the end, as he will now be blacklisted and unable to receive any more goods.

Sometimes, you may feel that a customer has completely ignored proper instructions. If you cave in to the complaint, you risk opening the flood gates to other unjustified complaints. A better course is to stand firm and politely point out that the product was not used for the purpose intended. After all, the product is being called into question and to offer any recompense may be interpreted as an admission that the product is at fault.

The evidence needs to be irrefutable, as here, when warnings are given in the instruction manual about which materials the drill is suitable for and which it is not. Note how the line of evidence is separated out from the rest of the text, since it is the crux of the argument. Emboldening it heightens the eye's attention to it. The door is shut firmly in the customer's face with the phrase "...I regret that we are unable to assist you further in this matter", a wonderfully polite and understated way of saying 'get lost' without causing offence.

IDENDEN INDUSTRIES
A division of Idenden Plc
Porter House, Hull HU7 4RF England

Tel 01482 119087 Fax 01482 119088
Registered in England No: 1218943

Mr D Redwood
Cedar Cottage
Little Lane
Wass
York
YO9 6TG

3 February 1999

Dear Mr Redwood,

I have considered your letter of 21st January and your assertion that our K31 power drill does not fulfil the claims made for it.

In your letter you maintain that this drill was used by you as directed, in the construction of a new extension to your house, as a result of which the motor burnt out only a month after the expiry of the guarantee. A telephone call to you from one of our staff subsequently revealed that you used this drill with a large masonry bit, for drilling into concrete.

I feel that I should point out that our K31 model is an *excellent* drill for the purposes for which it is sold, that is, for light jobs around the home. This point is made quite clearly in the instruction manual which come with your drill, in particular at the bottom of section two "Suitable Material" where it states:

"This drill is not suitable for heavy-duty drilling in materials such as concrete."

Much more suitable would be one of our K80 or K90 range, in that they have more robust motors as well as an impact facility, normally expected for drilling into materials such as concrete. The K31 boasts no such facility.

For these reasons I regret, therefore, that I cannot agree with your assertion.

Since your guarantee has expired, and since your drill has been used for purposes **specifically** stated as unsuitable, I regret that we are unable to assist you further in this matter.

Yours sincerely,

Frank Pillow
Customer Services Director

B & R HENDERSONS LTD
Marlows Road, Aberdeen AB20 5GT
Tel: 01224 267855 Fax: 01224 267977
Reg. No: 16497811 VAT No: 7387945

Helen Mitchell
Sales Manager
Good & Peabody
34 Kiln Street
Aberdeen
Scotland
AB8 7HY

13 August 1999

Dear Helen,

Re: Order Numbers 112568 and 112572

I am afraid that our Financial Director has put these orders on hold, due to payment problems. He faxed your office last week regarding the two overdue payments, but he has had no reply.

I have processed your orders, since I want them to be ready for despatch as soon as I am authorised to release them. However, this will not happen until the problem is resolved. Is there anything you can do?

I look forward to hearing from you.

Regards

Yours sincerly

Tina Cox
Sales Manager

A situation in which orders are stopped because of non-payment is usually battled out between the two financial departments of the businesses. The sales and customer-services departments will become involved if there are orders pending.

Here, a friendly letter is sent mainly to inform the customer that payments are overdue. Both parties know it is not directly their responsibility but the appeal in the closing line: "Is there anything you can do?" is designed to influence the customer into taking action. The sender emphasises his own efficiency (contrasted with the customer's inefficiency) by saying that the next orders are ready to be despatched. A good, friendly, influential letter.

Some customers may try to abuse your terms and conditions. It can be tricky – do you risk losing a potential customer or allow yourself to be taken advantage of? The solution here is to take a firm line and point out politely how far your terms and conditions have been exceeded.

Note the technique designed to show how reasonable you are. The supplier achieves this by saying that he doesn't mind that one of his conditions has been exceeded; the real objection is to the condition in which the shirt has been returned.

H J KINGSLEY (NORWICH) LTD

Kingsley House, Morris Street, Norwich NR6 7JM
Tel: (01603) 117097 Fax: (01603) 117099 Reg. No: England 12086215 VAT No: 8793519

Mr Lester Patterson
30 Virgin Close
Doncaster
S Yorks
DN9 0DB

26 May 1999

Dear Mr Patterson,

I am writing concerning your request for a refund on the shirt which you purchased from us.

As you know, under our conditions of sale, we offer all our customers a ten-day, no-quibble, money-back guarantee, provided the goods are returned within this period in a saleable condition.

We despatched your parcel to you on 15 March. The parcel in which you returned the item to us was date stamped 16 May. Even allowing five days for our parcel to reach you, this means that you have had the goods in your possession for 56 days, some 41 days outside our guarantee period. While we would be willing to overlook this point, we were concerned to find that the shirt you returned had clearly been worn and was soiled to an extent that it cannot be offered for resale.

I very much regret, therefore, that we shall be unable to offer you a refund. I am returning the shirt to you under separate cover.

Yours sincerely

P Phillips
Customer Services Manager

Grange & Turner Ltd

32 WESTBOURN ROAD, WITNEY, OXON OX6 7HY

Telephone (01993) 107888
Fax (01993) 107843

Reg. No: England 13078453
VAT No: 75698764

Ms Olive Short
Purchasing Manager
Parker Bright Ltd
72 Dudley Road
Brighton
Essex
BR6 5RT

13 March 1999

Dear Ms Short

Thank you for your letter of 7th March, which reached me today.

It was very kind of you to take the trouble to write to say how our service has helped you. As I am sure you are aware it is always very uplifting to be thanked - and I find letters of thanks when we haven't done anything 'special', just gone about providing our normal service, the most pleasant of all.

How do we seem to match your needs?

Firstly, there is quite a lot of choice. Approximately 30 new products are introduced each month, roughly one hundred different products in the course of a year. So there is good chance of meeting the need of the moment of each individual person.

But secondly, and much more importantly, it is the market that ultimately selects the products. It is the products that sell well (and are not returned under our guarantee) that stay in the leaflets. In fact, they have been voted for by other customers. The needs of one customer are often very like the need of another.

So we don't need a mole in your business – we just have to watch what everyone else wants! Of course, we make the initial choice, but even this is based on years of experience of what it is that makes a bestselling product that everybody wants to buy.

Once again, thank you very much indeed for taking the trouble to write to me.

Yours sincerely

Herbert Short
Manager

Customers' letters of thanks are some of the best (although often the rarest) letters to receive in business. When they do come, you should not ignore them. Instead, you should respond, reaffirming in the customer's mind that you are a good company to be doing business with.

The style of this letter is good because it takes a modest approach by saying "...we haven't done anything 'special'...". The closing line has a nice ring to it, showing the real appreciation that is felt for the letter. The customer cannot fail to think this is a business worth dealing with.

When writing letters of thanks, it is always nice if you thank, not just the person you are writing to, but also to ask for your thanks to be passed on to other people you met.

Saying something appreciative which engenders a positive feeling, for example, how your expectations were exceeded, is another useful tip for earning credit with the customer. This is done here with the declaration that the company is ahead of the game in fields other than 'systems'.

Charles Cunningham Ltd

29 Baker Street, LONDON N34 6GH England
Tel: (0171) 015 1290 Fax: (0171) 015 1271
Reg. No: England 1104398135 VAT No: 82108643

Ms Debra Clifton
Vice President
Winger & Ewing Inc.
7853 Wateridge Drive
Pleasanton
CA 95488
USA

24 May 1999

Dear Deb,

Having arrived safely back in the UK and having adjusted to the time difference, the size of the place and the fact that coffee is served at the end of meals, I am now in a position to write to you concerning our visit to your offices.

Firstly, I would like to say thank you to you and all your colleagues for the wonderful hospitality and the time you were willing to devote to our visit. We would be grateful if you would thank your colleagues on our behalf.

We were very impressed with the obvious professionalism that runs throughout your organisation. Having been told that you were "the number one for systems"; not only was this confirmed but, our impression is, that you are excellent at all the other aspects as well.

All this leaves to say is thank you once again for your hospitality; I hope we will have the opportunity to respond in a similar fashion if you, or any of your colleagues, visit the UK.

With kind regards,

Yours sincerely,

D. Dean
Director

Grange & Turner Ltd

32 WESTBOURN ROAD, WITNEY, OXON OX6 7HY

Telephone (01993) 107888
Fax (01993) 107843

Reg. No: England 13078453
VAT No: 75698764

Mr D Drake
24 Berry Green
Wellingborough
Northants
NN43 5MN

12 August 1999

Dear Mr Drake

Thank you very much indeed for your extremely pleasant letter, which arrived this morning. It brightened my day very considerably.

I do not know whether you can imagine how very encouraging it is in a mail-order company to get letters of appreciation (most people are moved to write only to complain!). And of course there is even greater pleasure in restoring a damaged relationship with a long-standing customer.

Thank you very much indeed for taking the trouble to write to reassure me. Please do let me know if anything goes wrong again.

Yours sincerely

Thomas Griffiths
Director

This letter shows how, even though the sender, Thomas Griffiths, doesn't know Mr Drake, a friendly, informal tone can be struck. It is even better, because the customer, who had vowed (in an earlier letter) never to have anything more to do with the business after a hiccup in the customer-service system, was won back by a highly personalised letter explaining what went wrong.

Asking the reader to imagine how encouraging it is to receive this type of letter has the effect of pulling the customer closer – getting him to empathise with your situation – and build the common bond you have.

The enthusiasm shines through in the use of adjectives designed to emphasise the genuine feeling of pleasure: "...your extremely pleasant letter..."; "...very considerably..."; "...even greater pleasure...", which all add up to a great sense of warmth.

This is one of those 'just keeping in touch' letters that is not absolutely necessary but is often welcomed by the recipient.

It can be quite a shock to 'phone a company, only to be told that the person you wish to speak to has left. Letters like this also benefit customers and suppliers, because they are kept informed about who to contact. If a new contact-name is not given, the customer may feel that your company isn't concerned to communicate with him, so why should he keep doing business with you, even though such claims may be totally unjustified.

If a lot of the goodwill in the relationship is tied up in the personal nature of the contact, it is worth bringing into the letter a comment expressing your confidence in the continuing relationship after you have left.

Wright & Simpson

157 Colder Way
Basingstoke
Hants RG21 5TG
Tel: (01256) 125907
Fax: (01256) 190986

Mr Robin Gillett
Marketing Director
Taylor Jones Ltd
23 Green St
Liverpool
L17 6HY

28 July 1999

Dear Robin,

Just a quick note to let you know that I have successfully completed my assignment at Wright and Simpson and will be taking up my new position as Director of International Business with Jackson Powell on 10th August.

I believe that Wright and Simpson has once again regained its position as one of the leading training consultancies and I am pleased to have been associated with this success.

It is also my pleasure to advise you that the General Manager's position will be filled in-house by Graham Fox; and he will be assisted by John Birch and Sheila Cox, who will be responsible for enquiries and order-processing respectively.

It has been a pleasure working with you and I am confident you will continue to enjoy a long and successful association with Wright and Simpson.

Best regards

Yours sincerely

Stuart Davis
Consultant

Partners: EG Wright MA & FA Simpson

H J KINGSLEY (NORWICH) LTD

Kingsley House, Morris Street, Norwich NR6 7JM
Tel: (01603) 117097 Fax: (01603) 117099 Reg. No: England 12086215 VAT No: 8793519

Ms Gail Wilson
Marketing Manager
Bridgewater Bright Ltd
76 Chalmers Way
Andover
Hants
SP4 7JK

28 September 1999

Dear Gail,

In conversation with your colleague Mary yesterday, it emerged that you have not had up-to-date information from us recently on our range of products. So I am putting that right immediately.

As promised, I am enclosing our newly revised catalogue, which brings you right up to date with our new products and innovations.

At the front of the catalogue are the most recent acquisitions, with a breakdown of their key features. The bestsellers follow and I am certain these will be familiar to you. At the back, we have more specialist topics, some of which are esoteric enough for the most confirmed devotees. I hope these will be of interest to you.

If you would like further information, please ring us on (01603) 117097 or fax us on (01603) 117099.

Best wishes,

Yours sincerely

Nina Davis
Marketing Manager

You may run into an old acquaintance with whom you used to do business. You would like to reawaken that business relationship. This letter attempts to bridge the gap, with a copy of the latest catalogue.

Note how the writer draws the reader's attention to the content of the catalogue, not just the fact there is a catalogue. This device tries to tempt the reader to turn the page – and to stop them from putting the catalogue to one side.

CHAPTER THREE

Debt Collection and Credit Control

Chasing for payment can be a soul-destroying activity, as customers either try to wriggle out of paying at all, or test your patience by seeing how long they can go without having to pay up. Many of the letters in this chapter are proven winners at getting recalcitrant customers to dig deep into their pockets and pay their dues. So you can be confident about using them, knowing that they have been genuinely tried and tested.

Choosing the right tone

Hitting the right note, first time, in a letter demanding payment, is not always easy. To help you choose, the collection letters have been divided broadly into three areas, as the Contents show: straightforward first-time demands for payment (letters 38–39); stronger demands (letters 40–41) and final demands that choose sterner phrases (letters 42–43).

Incentives and deterrents

If you want to try to avoid sending a letter chasing payment, the section on granting credit (letters 44 and 45) shows a letter opening an account and one offering an incentive for prompt payment.

Queries and disputes

Sorting these out need not always be a headache. Letters 48 and 49 show how to handle them successfully.

Handling a demand for payment

If you find yourself on the receiving end of a demand for payment, letter 50 should help to keep the pack at bay for a little longer.

This is an initial letter chasing payment. Its sole purpose is to exact confirmation of when payments will be forthcoming. Note how the tone is completely neutral and unhostile. Laying out the outstanding items in a table, giving relevant dates, invoice references, details of what was purchased and the value of each invoice, will help prevent the company from claiming that they can't find the information.

RPP Holdings Plc
35/38 New Road, Paignton, Devon TQ3 4UU
Tel: 01803 175653 Fax: 01803 187908
Reg. No: England 1976143

Fax Message to:	Maurice Brown Manilla Stationery Ltd
Fax Number:	0171 189 2008
From:	Tom Richards, Financial Director
Date:	31st July 1999

Listed below are open items on your account that I believe are past their due date for payment. Please confirm when each will be paid.

Manilla Stationery Ltd - Sales Account History

Tp	Date	Ref	Details	Amount
SI	03.03.99	20331	M/R continuous computer paper	£214.73
SI	10.03.99	20334	DL envelopes Non-window S/S	£522.00
SI	03.04.99	20354	M/R continuous computer paper	£864.23
SI	21.04.99	20362	A4 Photocopier paper	£442.00

Total due:	**£2042.96**

Regards

Tom Richards
Finance Director

THIS MESSAGE CONSISTS OF 1 PAGE. PLEASE LET US KNOW BY PHONE OR FAX IMMEDIATELY IF ANY PAGE IS ILLEGIBLE.

SIMPSON & MARTIN

39 TOP STREET
STOKE-ON-TRENT
ST2 3DR UNITED KINGDOM
Tel: (01782) 156232 Fax: (01782) 120899
Reg. No: England 96223978 VAT No: 91210674

Mr Frank Little
Finance Director
P G Black Ltd
Turner Way
Denton
Peterborough
PE6 8HJ

26 May 1999

Dear Mr Little,

Thank you for the business which you have brought to us; we've invoiced you almost £10,786.56 since the beginning of our financial year (August). We haven't met, but I look after the money at Simpson & Martin.

It's always pleasing to see new business - but even more pleasing to be paid for that business. And it is this thorny issue of payment that causes me to write to you.

Four orders have been accepted on "Mailing Date plus 60 days" credit and subsequent orders have been accepted on "Mailing Date plus 30 days" credit. This means that we expect to receive payment within, respectively, 60 and 30 days of the mailing date. But this has, so far, not happened.

We expected to receive a payment at the end of March for your orders 115684 and 115712 (see attached account history). And we expected two further payments to follow.

We did finally receive a payment on 12 May. But we have had no advice from your accounts to say which invoices are being paid or what the gross amount transmitted was, and the amount received does not tally with any combination of outstanding invoices.

In the interim, more invoices have fallen due for payment. Please confirm to me that these will be paid promptly and that future business will be conducted as expected.

I look forward to hearing from you.

Yours sincerely

William Patterson
Finance Director

With new trading partners, you can never tell what the payment record is going to be like. This one adopts a rather prickly tone. The line at the end of the first sentence: "I look after the money at Simpson & Martin" is designed to emphasise that this is not a standard chasing letter but about a more serious issue. The prickly feeling is enhanced in the second paragraph, with the metaphor: "...this thorny issue of payment...".

The organised way in which the Finance Director knows exactly which payments are meant to be made at what time contrasts with the chaotic payment received, suggesting that the customer's is not in order. The goal here is to make it quite clear to the the trading partner that you are aware of what is going on and so encourage them into a more timely payment pattern, before alternative action becomes imperative.

This chaser is a fairly pleasant example of a final demand. Referring to the series of chasing faxes and telephone call acts as a reminder of how much effort you have exerted, without response.

Note how the amount outstanding and account number are outside the main body of the text, the implication being that everyone knows what is outstanding.

Giving the bank details again will pre-empt any excuses that this information is missing. The phrase at the end of the fax "...in view of the one-sided nature of our correspondence..." adds a touch of mordant wit that should increase the embarrassment of the recipient as well as slightly drawing the sting of the serious threat to begin legal action against him.

Thomas King & Palmer Ltd

serving the world

24 Fuller Road, Welling,
Kent DA16 7JP
Tel : (01322) 100132
Fax : (01322) 100178

Reg. No : England 1212298762
VAT No : 92905643

Facsimile Cover Sheet

To: Peter Johnson
Company: Peter Johnson Inc.
Phone: 00 1 505 171 623
Fax: 00 1 505 171 698

From: James Steven
Company: Thomas King & Palmer
Phone: 01322 100132
Fax: 01322 100178

Date: 7 November 1999
No of Pages: 1

Please let us know by phone or fax immediately if any page is missing or has been garbled in transmission.

Amount outstanding: £2658.89   Account number: PL98358

I have now sent you a number of fax messages and spoken personally to you on the telephone (on 1 October).

My most recent fax was sent on 25 October. I am disappointed to have had no response to it.

Please will you arrange immediate payment of the amount due to our bankers:-

RSH Bank,
Main Street, Welling (Sort Code 10-12-13)
For account of: Thomas King & Palmer, Account No.3
Account number: 26479310

If we have not received payment within seven days then, in view of the one-sided nature of our correspondence, I can see no option but to seek the assistance of attorneys to resolve the situation.

Yours sincerely

James Steven
Financial Manager

H J KINGSLEY (NORWICH) LTD

Kingsley House, Morris Street, Norwich NR6 7JM
Tel: (01603) 117097 Fax: (01603) 117099 Reg. No: England 12086215 VAT No: 8793519

FAX MESSAGE TO: Jim Clements Copy to Accounts Dept

FAX No: 01654 789654

FROM :   Tim Good, Financial Director   DATE: 6 July 1999

THIS MESSAGE CONSISTS OF ONE PAGE. PLEASE LET ME KNOW BY PHONE OR FAX IMMEDIATELY IF ANY PAGE IS ILLEGIBLE.

Our Invoice No. SP56732
In April this year you ordered, a shrink-wrapping machine from us: Order No 115682, placed by Jim Clements.

Payment on our invoice (no. SP56732, copy follows) for this order was due 30 days from invoice date - i.e. 31 May 1999.

I have sent faxes to both yourself and to your accounts department, asking for confirmation that the invoice has been received and that it will be paid. It is now several months overdue.

To date I have had no reply.

We supply to valued customers in good faith and on the understanding that what we supply will be paid for. It is somewhat disconcerting when we endeavour to communicate with a customer regarding payment and are met with a wall of silence.

Please arrange for immediate payment direct to our bankers:
RSH Bank Plc – England
Sort Code: 00 12 34
Account Name: HJ Kingsley (Norwich) Ltd
Account No: 978164978

I look forward to receiving confirmation of payment and to a long, fruitful and communicative business relationship.

Yours sincerely

Tim Good
Finance Director

Threats are omitted from this letter but the message is just as potent. The customer's sense of fair play and common courtesy is called into question, by the perfectly reasonable request that 'we are only trying to talk to you'.

The last sentence should strike a chord – the implication being that a failure to pay will mean your services being withdrawn. The 'wall of silence' idea is echoed in the request for a 'communicative' business relationship in the final sentence.

This is a stern but, on the whole, polite letter. It gives the recipient an opportunity to give a reason why payment is being withheld. It is interesting because the other hands into which this case will be put, if payment is not received, are "collection agents", which somehow has a slightly more sinister tone than lawyers. It conjures up images of the men in dark coats being sent round to sort things out. Another interesting feature is the closing line. This phrase "...please disregard this letter..." is usually found in correspondence with consumers (rather than other businesses) but it is useful if you don't want to appear more heavy-handed than is absolutely necessary.

B & R Hendersons Ltd
Marlows Road, Aberdeen AB20 5GT
Tel: 01224 267855 Fax: 01224 267977
Reg. No: 16497811 VAT No: 7387945

Mr A Scott
General Manager
Scott Bros
Morton House
Station Road
Glasgow
G6 7HY

13 September 1999

Dear Mr Scott

Account No: 527BSGPR
Post Date: 10.07.99
Outstanding amount: £21.86

Your account with us is now SERIOUSLY OVERDUE. Should you have any justification for withholding payment, we would be obliged to hear from you concerning the problem.

However, if we do not hear from you by return or receive payment for the above account within the next seven days, you will leave us no alternative but to instruct our Collection Agents to take sufficient action to secure the amount outstanding.

We would very much regret having to take this decision and suggest that you immediately make the necessary arrangement for payment.

If you have sent your remittance in the last few days, please disregard this letter.

Yours sincerely,

Jane Fuller
Credit Controller

GKT Products Ltd, Unit 10, Castleway Lane, Alloway, Ayr, KA7 4BE
Telephone (01292) 177900 Fax (01292) 199855   Reg. No: 17964583 VAT No: 679845

Mr T Freeborn
Managing Director
F & G (Packaging) Ltd
12 The Industrial Park
Morley Road
Dartford
Kent
DA1 2TH

12 November 1999

Dear Mr Freeborn

Account Number: 2698745
Amount Due: £4896.89

This account has now been passed into legal hands. We will issue
Court proceedings against you seven days from the date of this
letter, unless before then we receive a cheque for this sum.

There will be no further warning. The proceedings will include
additional claims for legal costs and statutory interest resulting from
your prior failure to pay. Upon judgment we will forthwith execute
against you.

If we are not placed in full funds within the above time limit, we
reserve the right alternatively, where grounds exist, to instruct our
Solicitors to issue the relevant petition under the Insolvency Act
1986.

We look forward to your immediate remittance.

Yours sincerely

For & on behalf of
GKT Products Ltd
Legal Department

If you send this type of letter you must be certain about carrying out your threat. Some unscrupulous companies may decide to call your bluff and test your threat before deciding to settle.

This letter has got past the threatening stage. Its power lies in the double implication that they will not only take you to court to recover the sum but also consider winding your company up.

This letter starts an account on a firm, business-like basis. Four key points are worth noting and including in similar letters: an opportunity for the account holder to correct any errors in the address details; their attention drawn to the terms and conditions of sale and their point of contact in the sales department named. The most important piece of information, the credit limit and terms, is given prominence in the heart of the letter. Note that the word 'concurrent' is used here, to prevent the other party from running up invoices that exceed £1500 until it has paid the amount due within the 30-day period.

H J KINGSLEY (NORWICH) LTD

Kingsley House, Morris Street, Norwich NR6 7JM
Tel: (01603) 117097 Fax: (01603) 117099 Reg. No: England 12086215 VAT No: 8793519

Mr L Evans
Purchasing Manager
Parker Glass Ltd
Unit 27 Willow Park
Christchurch
Dorset
BH23 6MM

27 April 1999

Dear Mr Evans

Thank you for your application for a credit account. We have pleasure informing you that your account is now open; your account number is 013649780.

Please check the above address details and inform us of any amendments.

A credit limit of £1500 has been fixed to your account, concurrent to our 30 days net credit terms. Subject to your payments reaching us on the said date and your adherence to our terms, we will review your credit status on application.

If you have any queries regarding our conditions of sale, they can be found on the reverse of most of our documentation. Additionally, our accounts department will be more than pleased to advise you.

Your Area Sales Manager, Mr Thomas Carter, has been informed that your account is now open.

Yours sincerely

Rose Adams
Accounts Administrator

IDENDEN INDUSTRIES
A division of Idenden Plc
Porter House, Hull HU7 4RF England

Tel 01482 119087 Fax 01482 119088
Registered in England No: 1218943

Michael North
Sales Director
Beta Engineering Co
Silver Street
Foxhill
Swindon
SN3 7NM

30 May 1999

Dear Mr North

Please find enclosed our statement as at 31 July for £2903.86.

We have pleasure in offering a prompt payment discount with this invoice of £87.12. To claim it, our account must be credited with the full amount of £2816.74 within seven working days of the date of this invoice, otherwise I regret we must ask you to pay £2903.86.

We look forward to receiving your payment.

Yours sincerely

John Goodge
Finance Director

This request adopts a formal tone but is nonetheless quite friendly. On most occasions it would be unusual to enclose a letter with a statement. If you are suggesting a special arrangement, or this is a new benefit which you are introducing for the first time, it is worth enclosing a letter drawing it to the customer's attention.

If you sell low-cost items that would take a lot of administrative time in credit control, it is probably not worth giving credit on the items unless your customers are regular buyers. Here, the product costs only £32.90. If the debtor decided to delay payment, any profit on the sale would soon be swallowed up in having to send collection letters. With the certainty of payment in advance, you can be confident that your profit remains intact.

H J KINGSLEY (NORWICH) LTD

Kingsley House, Morris Street, Norwich NR6 7JM
Tel: (01603) 117097 Fax: (01603) 117099 Reg. No: England 12086215 VAT No: 8793519

Mr G Johnson
General Manager
Taylor & Ball
25 South Lane
Norwich
NR4 5EK

16 June 1999

Dear Mr Johnson

Your order no. FG6799
Thank you for the above order.

We enclose our pro forma invoice no. SD2495 for £32.90.

When we receive your remittance, the goods will be despatched to you the same day.

Yours sincerely

Barry Fuller
General Manager

Grange & Turner Ltd

32 WESTBOURN ROAD, WITNEY, OXON OX6 7HY

Telephone (01993) 107888
Fax (01993) 107843

Reg. No: England 13078453
VAT No: 75698764

Mr A Scott
General Manager
Scott Bros
Morton House
Station Road
Glasgow
G6 7HY

13 September 1999

Dear Mr Scott

I am writing to you because I want you to know of our experience when attempting to be paid on agreed terms by your company.

Names are rented by your company from our mailing lists department. Terms agreed, and signed by your company secretary, are "30 days", i.e. payment is due at the end of the month following that in which the invoice is issued.

Yet repeatedly we are told by your accounts department that the terms are 60 days. Colleagues have phoned and spoken to the people who place the orders with us and carefully reminded them of the agreed terms. And yet nothing changes.

On 17 April, I 'phoned to request payment for a February invoice. I was told "we pay on 60 days". That day I wrote to Helen Winters, who had placed the order.

Today, having had no reply, I phoned her – to be told that she has left. And when I spoke to the accounts person, I was told that "a cheque will be put in the post today".

Despite all those previous conversations, 78 days from the date of our invoice, on agreed terms of 30 days, your cheque has not even been mailed. I wonder when it would have been?

Given this experience I am sure that you will understand when I say that I can no longer make credit facilities available to your company. Any future orders will have to be paid for in advance.

Yours sincerely,

Jane Markham
Finance Director

The tone of this letter is stern, with an undercurrent of irritation. The customer is playing the old game of ignoring agreed terms and paying when he feels like it. Listing the sequence of events (showing yourself as being completely reasonable and the customer's accounts department as completely unreasonable) gives greater weight to your actions when you announce that credit is being withdrawn.

Note how the supplier defines the credit terms of "...30 days...". This is important, because some companies mean literally 30 days from the date of the invoice, while others mean (as here) at the end of the month following that in which the invoice is issued. Another effective technique is use of the rhetorical question in the penultimate paragraph "I wonder when it would have been?", which underlines your lack of trust in the customer.

Setting your debts to a business against theirs to you, is another trick accounts departments like to play.

The difficulty with this arrangement (as highlighted here) is that, unless the trades are simultaneous and the payment terms identical, it means that one side inevitably obtains more credit than the other. No wonder someone is going to cry 'foul'.

Highlighting how many days it has taken for payments to arrive (or not to arrive) is another smart technique to use. The precision accentuates the point and creates a stronger impact than simply saying that payment is 'overdue'.

SIMPSON & MARTIN

39 TOP STREET
STOKE-ON-TRENT
ST2 3DR UNITED KINGDOM
Tel: (01782) 156232 Fax: (01782) 120899

Reg. No: England 96223978 VAT No: 91210674

FAX MESSAGE TO: Brian Johnson
ALF Services Limited
Maid House, West Road, Reading
Fax No: 01753 956717

From: William Patterson   Date: 1.10.99

Re Overdue Invoices

I was astonished when I telephoned your accounts department this morning to enquire when our July invoices would be paid, to be invited to accept setting them against your invoices to us not yet due. I thought that it was only fair that you were put in the picture.

I have sent the following message to Tracey Macer, who requested this:-

"Here is a copy of our order No 101687, which resulted in your invoice D4/09210 and credit D40931. You will see that terms agreed with Brian Johnson included payment '30 days from mailing date'."

The relevant mailing date was 15.09.99. Payment is not yet due.

The payment which I am requesting from ALF is for invoices dated 11.7.99. According to the terms signed by ALF (copy follows) payment was due 30 days later. Today, 82 days later, we have not been paid.

You have asked me to accept setting Simpson & Martin's debt to ALF against ALF's debt to Simpson & Martin. This I cannot accept. ALF's debt is very much overdue, whilst Simpson & Martin's is not yet due.

I reserve the right to treat agreed credit terms in the same way ALF treats them.

I would be grateful if you would arrange immediate payment of your overdue account with us.

ALF's history of payment is not brilliant. In the last year it has taken more than 100 days for us to be paid for some invoices.

Regards

William Patterson
Finance Director

IDENDEN INDUSTRIES
A division of Idenden Plc
Porter House, Hull HU7 4RF England

Tel 01482 119087 Fax 01482 119088
Registered in England No: 1218943

Jim Little
Marketing Director
York Plastics
54 East Street
York
YO9 8BM

22 February 1999

Dear Jim,

We have recently received the enclosed statement from you.

We are at a loss to know why this should have been re-issued, as the sum in question was paid directly to your bankers from our bank on 19th February 1999. I enclose a copy of the advice from our bank.

I hope this matter can now be considered closed.

Yours sincerely

John Goodge
Finance Director

Occasionally, you may find that statements are accidentally duplicated. (It can be surprising how many companies who receive a duplicate invoice actually pay it as well!) This letter should sort matters out.

Note the way this letter closes. This is a useful phrase that can be applied in any situation where you want to signal that you don't expect to hear from the supplier's accounts department again.

If you find yourself on the receiving end of an irate creditor on the warpath for their money, this letter should help to appease him.

Note how the 'reasons' are very conveniently side-stepped, with an all-embracing phrase (which could be used on a multitude of occasions) that explains they are "...both tedious and convoluted." A super phrase that says absolutely nothing but will leave the other side with the impression of a good story left untold.

The last sentence should help to restore the creditor's faith in you; implying the invoice "...slipped through the net..." makes it sound like a one-off mishap.

Taylor Taylor & Shaw
Benton House, Clifton, Bristol BS16 7LJ
Tel: (0117) 1089254   Fax: (0117) 1089211

FAX MESSAGE

To: Sally White

Fax No: 0181 756 9841

From: Peter Pope   Date: 23 June 1999

THIS MESSAGE CONSISTS OF ONE PAGE. PLEASE LET ME KNOW BY PHONE OR FAX IMMEDIATELY IF ANY PAGE IS ILLEGIBLE.

Dear Ms White.

Re: Your Fax of 7 June 1999
First, apologies for the delay in replying to your fax, which was caused by the absence of Michael Taylor and myself on business travel overseas.

Your invoice no. CP25648 will be settled in full on Monday, when we should have received a corresponding cheque from Ferdinand Ramos of Marco Leathers Inc., which has been couriered to us from their offices in the Philippines today.

The reasons for the delay are both tedious and convoluted. Suffice it to say, your cheque will be despatched by express air mail on Monday, with a copy sent to you by fax to confirm despatch.

Should any future invoices 'slip through the net', please do not hesitate to bring it to my personal attention and I will attempt to resolve the problem immediately.

Regards

P Pope
Financial Manager

Partners: AW Taylor & GS Taylor

CHAPTER FOUR

Employing People

A scan of the letters contained in this chapter shows the diversity of employee-related subjects that demand correspondence. Some of them are fairly straightforward, such as asking a candidate to attend an interview. Others, such as warnings and dismissals, require more consideration to make sure the correct legal regulations are being adhered to satisfactorily. All of them need to be carefully drafted if they are not to be misinterpreted by the recipient. Some of the highlights are examined here.

References
Giving references can be awkward, because of the need to give a fair and honest reply which does not conceal relevant information. A failure to do this could expose you to a claim from either the prospective employer or the employee. Letter 55 illustrates how to handle the letter.

Giving warnings
Letters 57–9 cover the tricky issue of giving appropriate warnings to an employee about his or her conduct, from first written warning through to dismissal.

Congratulations
Offering appropriate congratulations can sometimes be as awkward as writing a letter of condolence. Letters 66 and 67 show how you can write a sincere and well-phrased letter.

It is a good practice to confirm all meetings in writing. It can be easy to mishear a time or date over the 'phone, or to be distracted soon after a 'phone call is finished and forget to make a note of it in a diary.

You don't need to write a long letter – a brief note containing the date, time and place will suffice. It is simple but it can save a lot of time and embarrassment later.

 Kelso Limited
16 Abbots Road, Luton, Bedford MK44 7YT
Tel: (01234) 136953 Fax: (01234) 136422
Registered in England No: 9126719 VAT No: 91523489 76

Barry Hall
27 Steeple Drive
Hitchin
Herts
SG4 5HJ

21 January 1999

Dear Mr Hall,

This is to confirm our meeting at Abbots Road, Luton at 1.00pm on 25 January 1999.

We look forward to seeing you then.

Yours sincerely

Faith Turner
Personnel Manager

SIMPSON & MARTIN

39 TOP STREET
STOKE-ON-TRENT
ST2 3DR UNITED KINGDOM
Tel: (01782) 156232 Fax: (01782) 120899
Reg. No: England 96223978 VAT No: 91210674

Miss T Hussey
16 Clover Terrace
Werrington
Stoke-on-Trent
ST9 0PL

3 January 1999

Dear Miss Hussey,

Thank you for your completed application form for the position of Word Processor Operator.

I am now considering all applications and will be in touch with you again within the next few days.

Yours sincerely

Elizabeth Bent
Personnel Officer

Before inviting a short-list of candidates to interview, you may want to give yourself time to consider all the applications. Candidates will be expecting to hear from you soon.

This letter helps to confirm that the application has been safely received and takes some of the anxiety out of the waiting. It doesn't raise any hopes that the applicant will be called for interview, nor does it dash them – it sits on the fence, leaving you with both options open.

This letter is a straightforward, formal rejection letter. Note how the letter doesn't give an explicit reason why the candidate has not been successful but just implies that though the applicant was a good candidate, there were others even better qualified.

The phrase "...I regret that we have decided not to take your application further on this occasion" is a little oblique, although its meaning is clear. When rejecting a candidate, make sure that your choice of words leaves the reader clear about where he stands. Try to avoid vague phrases that may be open to different interpretations.

H J KINGSLEY (NORWICH) LTD

Kingsley House, Morris Street, Norwich NR6 7JM
Tel: (01603) 117097 Fax: (01603) 117099 Reg. No: England 12086215 VAT No: 8793519

Mr M Booth
18 Woodgate St
East Dereham
NR19 6JH

22 January 1999

Dear Mr Booth

Thank you for attending the interview last week for the post of Office Manager.

The standard of applicants has been very high and, after careful consideration, I regret that we have decided not to take your application further on this occasion.

However, I would like to take this opportunity to thank you for the interest you have shown in our Company and to wish you every success in the future.

Yours sincerely

P J Cross
Personnel Manager

Charles Cunningham Ltd

29 Baker Street, LONDON N34 6GH England
Tel: (0171) 015 1290 Fax: (0171) 015 1271
Reg. No: England 1104398135 VAT No: 82108643

Mr Peter Holmes
Personnel Manager
Thomas King & Palmer
24 Fuller Road
Welling
Kent
DA16 2PL

3 March 1999

Dear Mr Holmes,

We have received an application from John Hibbert for the position of Office Manager.

I would be grateful if you could answer the questions below concerning John Hibbert's employment with you.

1. What date did he join and leave your company?
2. What job(s) did he perform at your company?
3. How would you rate his time-keeping?
4. How much time in a year did he take off for sickness?
5. How many people was he supervising in his job with you?
6. Has any disciplinary action had to be taken against him, however minor?
7. Would you say he is a conscientious worker?
8. How would you rate his experience to perform the job for which he has applied?
9. Are there any reasons that you are aware of why we should not employ him?
10. What was his reason for leaving your company?

Thank you for your help with this matter.

Yours sincerely

Sarah Milnes
Personnel Manager

When employing new staff, it is prudent to ask for a reference from their previous employer. This not only helps to verify that the candidate has worked where he says he did but it also gives you an opportunity to find out more about them.

The questions asked here should enable you to find out how well he worked for and was judged by his previous employer.

Asking for two references from different people means you have a chance to spot any inconsistent replies, which could signal a need for further questions or enquiries.

If you are asked to give a reference, it must be given honestly and fairly.

When giving a reference, you are in a position of privilege that entitles you to say exactly what you think about a person, even if it might, in other circumstances, be defamatory. However, you must not say anything about the person maliciously, otherwise the position of privilege may be lost and you could face a claim from the employee.

Similarly, a failure to answer a question truthfully may expose you to a claim from the employer. This sense of having to walk a fine line often leads to referees giving fairly anodyne, non-judgmental references. It would, therefore, be a mistake to treat the answers to a reference as telling all there is to know about an employee. Nevertheless, it does give a worthwhile snapshot view and acts as a useful check.

Thomas King & Palmer Ltd

serving the world

24 Fuller Road, Welling,
Kent DA16 7JP
Tel : (01322) 100132
Fax : (01322) 100178

Reg. No : England 1212298762
VAT No : 92905643

Sarah Milnes
Personnel Manager
Charles Cunningham Ltd
29 Baker Street
London
N34 6GH

8 March 1999

Dear Ms Milnes

Thank you for your request for a reference for John Hibbert.

I can confirm that John held the position of Office Assistant with us from June 1996 to April, 1998. In April, he was appointed Office Manager and he stayed with us until December of the same year.

John's time-keeping was excellent and, although he had the occasional day off sick in a year, the amount was no more than one would expect. Most of the occasions were caused by seasonal bouts of 'flu.

In his post of Office Assistant, no one reported to John. However, in his role of Office Manager, he was responsible for managing a team of six personal assistants.

No disciplinary action has ever been taken against John and he is a very conscientious worker.

I am not aware of all the responsibilities that you are expecting him to perform but, provided that they are broadly similar to those areas in which he has experience, I would say that he was well qualified to perform those tasks.

John told us he wished to leave because he was keen to work in a larger organisation, where there were greater opportunities for advancement and to learn more skills than we were realistically able to offer him.

I hope this gives you all the information you require but, if you do have any queries, please do not hesitate to contact me.

Yours sincerely

Peter Holmes
Personnel Manager

23 Gladstone Walk
Chepstow
Gwent
NP6 6LP

Mr G Moore
Managing Director
G B Grey Ltd
Church St
Newport
Gwent
NP9 7JW

19 May 1999

Dear Mr Moore,

It is with regret that I tender my resignation as Assistant Export
Manager. This follows my appointment as Export Manager with
Abeltech. As I am required under my contract to give one month's
notice, I understand my last day of employment will be 19th June 1999.

May I take this opportunity to thank you for all the invaluable help,
advice and encouragement that you have given me during my three
years with GB Grey. I have thoroughly enjoyed my time here but I feel
the moment is now right for me to take up new responsibilities and
challenges.

Yours sincerely

Peter King

A letter of resignation should be succinct and to the point. It is useful to specify the date that you intend to leave on, to avoid any misunderstanding later.

The second paragraph is not obligatory but helps set a friendly tone for the departure. It is always worth leaving on good terms. You never know when you may come into contact with the people for whom you work again, perhaps in other companies that you move to in the future.

This letter has a formal air to it. It is designed to confirm what has already been discussed at a previous meeting. It is also written to prevent any disagreement at a later stage about what action has or has not been taken.

It demonstrates that the company has done all it can to explain the importance of adhering to the safety regulations, should this be necessary at a future health and safety or industrial tribunal.

An interesting point to note is the way the letter seeks to win the employee back on to the side of the company by explaining that the code is not operated "...for the benefit of the company but for the benefit of all our employees", and "...one employee's breach of the code may endanger another employee's life".

IDENDEN INDUSTRIES
A division of Idenden Plc
Porter House, Hull HU7 4RF England

Tel 01482 119087   Fax 01482 119088
Registered in England No: 1218943

Mr Jack Turner
Welding Engineer

12 July 1999

Dear Mr Turner

Re: YOUR BREACH OF THE COMPANY'S SAFETY CODE

I confirm the points we discussed at our meeting on 12 July, concerning your negligence in adhering to the strict safety code we operate. The complaint was that on 12 July you did not wear a hard safety hat in the construction zone of the factory for a period of one hour.

As we agreed, you must at all times adhere to the safety code of the company. I am reissuing a copy of the code to you and am asking your manager to go through it with you again, so you are quite clear about what is expected of you. If you are unclear about anything, however trivial it may seem, do not hesitate to ask. The safety code of the company is not operated for the benefit of the company but for the benefit of all our employees. You must understand that one employee's breach of the code may endanger another employee's life and it is for this reason that we enforce the policy strictly.

We shall review the position in three months' time and, provided you have adhered to the safety code, no further action will be taken. I would like to make it clear though, that we expect you to follow that code strictly at all times.

Finally, please sign the enclosed copy of this letter to confirm that you have received this letter and another copy of the safety code and return it to me for my files.

Yours sincerely

John Cooper
Director of Personnel

IDENDEN INDUSTRIES
A division of Idenden Plc
Porter House, Hull HU7 4RF England

Tel 01482 119087 Fax 01482 119088
Registered in England No: 1218943

Mr Jack Turner
Welding Engineer

15 September 1999

Dear Mr Turner

Re: YOUR BREACH OF THE COMPANY'S SAFETY CODE
On 12 July, you breached the safety code by failing to wear a hard hat. On 15 September you were again discovered to have breached the code by not wearing the hard hat provided for you to use in the construction area of the factory.

It was made clear to you at the meeting on 12 July and in the letter to you of the same day that we expected you to follow the safety code strictly at all times. You have failed to do this.

For your own safety and for the safety of the others you must follow strictly all aspects of the safety code, especially wearing a hard hat in the zones required.

I must warn you that, because you have received previous warnings about your misconduct, if you fail to adhere to the safety standard again you will be dismissed.

Yours sincerely

John Cooper
Director of Personnel

The final letter is much colder in its approach. It makes it clear to the employee what the consequences will be of failing to adhere to the safety standard. There is no attempt to persuade the employee to cooperate for his own and others' sake.

Note how the letter refers to specific dates, confirming the history in case the matter should come to tribunal. The stern tone of "I must warn you..." cannot fail but to be understood by the reader.

The letter confirming dismissal sets out the events in a clear, factual way. It highlights the dates, to reinforce that the company has carried out its duties to the letter. It makes it clear that the company has given the employee the opportunity to improve his conduct, in case this should be used as a defence at an industrial tribunal.

Note how the letter omits any informal opening or closing sentence but instead leaps straight into the facts of the case and ends abruptly – appropriate for the serious tone that such a letter needs to adopt.

IDENDEN INDUSTRIES
A division of Idenden Plc
Porter House, Hull HU7 4RF England

Tel 01482 119087 Fax 01482 119088
Registered in England No: 1218943

Mr Jack Turner
Welding Engineer

27 October 1999

Dear Mr Turner

Re: YOUR BREACH OF THE COMPANY'S SAFETY CODE
On 27 October you were, for a third time, discovered not wearing a hard hat in the construction zone of the factory.

On 12 July and 15 September it was made clear to you that failure to wear a hard hat in a safety zone amounted to a breach of the company's safety code.

You were given a warning on 15 September that if you failed again to adhere to the company's safety code you would be dismissed.

You have been given the opportunity to improve your conduct but have repeatedly ignored these warnings given to you. In the circumstances we have no option but to dismiss you with effect from today. You will receive one month's pay in lieu of notice.

Yours sincerely

John Cooper
Director of Personnel

SIMPSON & MARTIN

39 TOP STREET
STOKE-ON-TRENT
ST2 3DR UNITED KINGDOM
Tel: (01782) 156232 Fax: (01782) 120899
Reg. No: England 96223978 VAT No: 91210674

Debra King
Sales Office

7 August 1999

Dear Debra,

Proposed Office Move

As you know, we have been working under cramped and sometimes difficult conditions, caused by the growth of our business. For several weeks we have been searching for new premises but, so far, nothing suitable has turned up and we have now retained an agency to look for an appropriate location.

Our first choice is to keep the business within the city centre but we are also looking at any location up to 25 miles outside the city boundary. One strict criterion is that any location outside the city centre must be on a suitable public transport route, to enable those of you who live within the city to travel with the minimum inconvenience.

This is as far as we have got in choosing a new location, but I will keep you informed, as and when developments occur.

Yours sincerely

Francis Vince
Managing Director

This is one of those letters that needs to be written to keep employees informed of a changing situation. You could announce this at a meeting or in a memo, but, occasionally, a letter may be appropriate. The aim must be to put people in the picture and stop any rumours that might be circulating. Employees often expect instant answers, which cannot always be given.

Here, the management go as far as they can to alleviate the concerns that employees may have about relocating, by explaining that they are trying to achieve a location within easy reach of the city.

When people leave, it is nice to announce the departure, to keep everyone informed. Again, a short note saying when the person is leaving and where they are moving to should be sufficient. A complimentary note about his achievements is always welcome, but make sure it is sincere and fitting for the person, otherwise it may be seen as, damning with faint praise'.

PARKER
Glass Ltd

Unit 27 Willow Park
Christchurch, Dorset BH23 6MM
Tel: 01202 109111
Fax: 01202 109112

Reg. No: England 962578762
VAT No: 9120564

1 May 1999

To all staff

Resignation of David Scannell

I am sorry to announce the resignation of David Scannell as Head of Sales.

David will be leaving us on 18th May and, after a short holiday, will be taking up his new position as Sales Director with Courtnay Breece Ltd. We shall be looking to appoint his successor within the next three to four weeks.

During the six years that he has been with us, David has presided over a growth in sales which has made us the envy of all our rivals. For this, and for his irrepressible good humour in the face of any crisis, he will be sadly missed.

There will be an opportunity for all staff to say farewell at a gathering at 1.30-2.30pm on 18th May in the Function Suite. Light refreshments will be available.

Peter Cox
Personnel Director

Charles Cunningham Ltd

29 Baker Street, LONDON N34 6GH England
Tel: (0171) 015 1290 Fax: (0171) 015 1271
Reg. No: England 1104398135 VAT No: 82108643

Mr David Hobbs
23 Heather Close
Cambridge
CB2 7HJ

25 January 1999

Dear David,

Company Loan

I am pleased to inform you that the Company agrees to make an interest-free loan available to you for £2566, so that you can purchase an annual season ticket for travel to and from work. The amount will be deducted from your salary in 12 equal monthly installments.

If, at any time during the course of the next 12 months, you leave the employment of the Company, you will be required to reimburse us for the outstanding amount of the loan.

I would be grateful if you could sign and date the enclosed form so that a cheque can be raised.

Yours sincerely

Kevin Gibson
Finance Manager

This letter is a standard company letter for all employees requiring a season-ticket loan. It has a matter-of-fact corporate tone that sticks to the essentials.

It is important, when writing these letters, not to omit details such as how the employee is expected to repay the amount to the company, and how any unused amounts of the loan must be reimbursed, if the employee leaves the company.

Terminating someone's contract is never pleasant but, if it can be done on amicable terms, so much the better. The employee and the employer in this case have mutually agreed to part company and the tone adopted is friendly and fits the occasion. It begins on an official note in the first paragraph but soon moves on to a more personal level.

The letter cleverly mixes compliments, praising the attributes of the employee, with a recognition that she does not have an aptitude for cold-calling which is always going to be "...an up-hill struggle for you". The phrases that praise are worth noting and include "...you would certainly be considered for such a post..." and "...we shall be only too happy to provide [a reference] for your satisfactory good character and conduct" which reinforce the good terms and mutually agreed nature of the termination.

⊗ WILSON SMITH LTD

A wholly-owned subsidiary of The Wilson Group PLC
16 Willow Walk, Retford, Nottingham NG6 8WS
Tel: (01777) 121211 Fax: (01777) 121233
Reg. No: England 1212298762

Ms Christine Edwards
24 Princes Avenue
Nottingham
NG4 7JU

10 September 1999

Dear Christine,

As we agreed this morning, I would like to confirm our mutual decision not to continue your employment beyond the end of next month. Your last day of employment will be 30 October.

I would not wish you to attribute any personal blame to the fact that we are not able to extend your contract beyond your three-month probationary period. The task of selling advertising space by telephone is never an easy one and, although you have made a determined effort, it seems that this field is always going to be an up-hill struggle for you. I certainly think that your suggestion of seeking a job in a marketing-oriented field, where there will be less cold-call selling, is likely to be more suited to your skills and aspirations. I only wish we had a vacancy for a marketing position here, as you would certainly be considered for such a post.

If you require a reference, we shall be only too happy to provide one for your satisfactory good character and conduct. You will understand that we would have to include in any reference the caveat that we would not consider cold-call telephone selling to be appropriate employment for you.

I would like to take this opportunity to wish you every success in your future.

Yours sincerely

Alice Pope
Marketing Director

Tyler & Piper Associates

76 Whites Lane, Stevenage, Herts SG1 8JP England
Tel: (01438) 186465 Fax: (01438) 164323

Mrs M Joseph
149 Bronsbury Park
Stevenage
Herts
SG1 7KJ

26 June 1999

Dear Mary,

Statutory Maternity Pay
Thank you for letting me know about your pregnancy – I am delighted for you and do hope everything goes well.

You asked whether you qualified for statutory maternity pay. I have checked the rules on this and they are as follows:

1. You must have been continuously employed by us for at least 26 weeks, continuing into the 15th week before the week your baby is due.

2. You must still be pregnant at the 11th week before the week the baby is due (or have had the baby by this time).

3. You must give us medical evidence of the date the baby is due at least 21 days before the maternity absence is due to start.

4. Your average weekly earnings must also not be less than the lower earnings limit for the payment of National Insurance, which I can confirm is the case in your instance.

You will receive maternity pay at 90 per cent of your average weekly earnings for the first six weeks in which it is due. Thereafter you will receive maternity pay at the standard rate for the following 12 weeks.

You have the right to return to work within 29 weeks of the birth of your baby, provided you give us 21 days written notice of the date you intend to return.

I hope this explains the position but if you have any other queries, please do ask.

Yours sincerely

Harry Law
Personnel Manager

Partners: DA Tyler BA & SR Piper MA

The rules concerning maternity leave are complex and should be checked carefully before a letter like this is written.

Given the complexity of the law and the need to assess each case individually, it is difficult not to sound too official when writing this letter, but the aim should be to include a mixture of congratulations with 'and these are the rules'.

The warm congratulatory tone is here reserved for the opening which helps to counteract the colder, more business-like message of the maternity-pay regulations.

Writing a letter that motivates is not easy. It must sound sincere, so the recipient takes it seriously. Money is only one way of rewarding people.

Here, money is not mentioned and instead, the writer capitalises on other motivational factors, such as recognition for a job well done: "...made such a positive contribution..."; rewarding with greater responsibility: "...I would like you to become fully responsible for..." and setting challenging goals to be attained: "...ensure that the targets which we have identified are achieved...".

Note how the person expresses confidence in the employee: "...I know you are very capable of accomplishing successfully".

Kelso Limited

16 Abbots Road, Luton, Bedford MK44 7YT
Tel: (01234) 136953 Fax: (01234) 136422
Registered in England No: 9126719 VAT No: 91523489 76

Mr J Edmonds
Despatch Department

29 June 1999

Dear James,

I think it was very useful to talk through your performance over the last six months and I wanted to confirm some of the points that were discussed. We are pleased with the way you have so quickly become a key member of the warehouse team and made such a positive contribution from the beginning. You are a conscientious worker and we are very keen for you to build upon the skills that you have developed so far.

As we discussed, from 1 July I would like you to become fully responsible for the following areas and ensure that the goals which we have identified are achieved.

Responsibility	Goal
1. Receive and check deliveries of new stock.	Same day unpacking, storage and notifying the relevant department of arrival.
2. Timely despatch of all goods.	75% of orders despatched the same day. The remainder to be despatched the following day.
3. Management of the warehouse.	Implement an efficient location and picking system for all stock.

I would like to monitor your performance on a monthly basis, to ensure that these targets are achieved and that any difficulties are ironed out at the earliest opportunity. I hope you enjoy the challenge that this role represents and which I know you are very capable of accomplishing successfully.

Yours sincerely

J Granger
General Manager

Charles Cunningham Ltd

29 Baker Street, LONDON N34 6GH England
Tel: (0171) 015 1290 Fax: (0171) 015 1271
Reg. No: England 1104398135 VAT No: 82108643

Ms Jan Hancock
Marketing Department

28 November 1999

Dear Jan,

Outstanding Employee of the Year Award 1999
I am delighted to confirm that you are this year's winner of
the Outstanding Employee of the Year Award.

The competition to achieve this accolade was considerable but
I am delighted to say that, although it was a very close-run
thing, your dedication to the task, combined with your
record-breaking output, were the winning factors that gave
you the edge over the other candidates.

I know that you have been a previous contender for the
position, and it is a tribute to your hard work and constancy
that, year after year, you have been able to turn out results
which anyone here would be proud of achieving.

It gives me great personal pleasure to recognise this
achievement with the accolade of the Outstanding Employee
of the Year and a well-earned prize of £500, which will be
added to your salary this month.

Congratulations, and I hope you will go on to defend your
title for many years to come.

Yours sincerely

T J Ward
Managing Director

The keynote here is to convey enthusiasm and echo the success and achievement that a winner of a performance award should feel.

You should always praise the achievement – this is one of the occasions when the management can freely give recognition, and it will be appreciated by the recipient. Try to make it as personal as possible, as in the phrase: "It gives me great personal pleasure to recognise...". Making the result seem close gives the impression that the competition was tough.

Note some of the phrases that are useful in similar letters: "...although it was a very close-run thing..."; "...it is a tribute to your hard work..." and "...a well-earned prize...".

Appreciating someone unexpectedly can be an extremely powerful tool for motivating them.

With performance awards, there is a sense that the appreciation is obligatory and slightly forced, because someone has to win. This can reduce the motivational benefit. But when a note of appreciation is unannounced and sincerely felt, its impact can be extremely rewarding.

This letter is a good example of the tone and feeling to aim for – particularly recognising areas where there was considerable resistance and achievements which, at the time, may have appeared to go unnoticed.

GKT Products Ltd, Unit 10, Castleway Lane, Alloway, Ayr, KA7 4BE
Telephone (01292) 177900 Fax (01292) 199855   Reg. No: 17964583 VAT No: 679845

David Holmes
General Manager

18 June 1999

Dear David,

The recent achievement of obtaining ISO 9001 has been one that the whole company has won by pulling together but, without the driving force of a few individuals firmly at the helm, I know the project would have had very little chance of even getting off the ground, let alone earning the rewards which are so richly deserved.

I recognise that, in the early stages of the project, you experienced considerable resistance to it from both management and employees alike. But, with your determination and hard work, you had the foresight to look ahead to today and convince all of us of the benefits we would be able to reap.

I know that this achievement is as much your special effort as it is the company's and I would like to say a very big personal 'thank you'. You have raised our profile in the eyes of our competitors, our parent company and amongst the other divisions. Well done.

Yours sincerely

Ron Blake
Director

GKT Products Ltd, Unit 10, Castleway Lane, Alloway, Ayr, KA7 4BE
Telephone (01292) 177900 Fax (01292) 199855   Reg. No: 17964583 VAT No: 679845

14 June 1999

To all members of staff

Health and Safety
Following the recent accident involving a visitor to our premises, I would like to remind everyone of our health and safety policy. A copy of the policy is attached. Please take two minutes to read it and remind yourself of the main points.

It is vital, for safety and security reasons, that if you have a visitor to the building you are responsible for them at all times. For his or her own safety he or she should not be allowed to wander freely around the building. Remember, the layout can be disorientating to visitors so, if your visitors need to use the toilets, do accompany them and escort them back.

For security reasons, if you should see someone you do not recognise wandering about the building unaccompanied, don't be afraid to ask them politely why he or she is here, whom the visitor is seeing and if that person knows the visitor has arrived.

All employees have a responsibility to take reasonable care of themselves and others and to achieve a healthy and safe workplace. If you notice any hazard or potential hazard do bring it to the attention of the Health and Safety Manager, John Fish, who will investigate the situation.

Thank you for your co-operation with this policy.

Yours sincerely

Karl Jones
Health & Safety Officer

Health and safety is often one of those areas that falls to the bottom of a company's list of priorities but every company must ensure they are complying adequately with the regulations. Health and Safety Inspectors are entitled to call unannounced. This letter aims to bring the topic to everyone's attention. It combines a further message about security issues, to prevent unwanted intruders. The tone is clear but fairly formal. "Please take two minutes to read it..." is a better way of saying 'please read it' as it suggests it will take a very short time and can be easily absorbed. More employees may be encouraged to take note of it instead of filing it away unread. Note the fairly emphatic tone used: "It is vital..."; "For their own safety..."; "...do accompany them..."; "For security reasons..."; "...don't be afraid to ask..." and "...do bring it to the attention of..." – each one designed to give everyone clear, unambiguous instructions.

Just as certain accidents and diseases have to be reported, so do deaths, even if they occur several months later, for example, following an accident.

The regulations require that the responsible person (usually the employer) notify the Health and Safety Executive by the quickest means practicable, which could be 'phone or fax. Initially you need only give the basic information – subsequently, a form giving more specific details will have to be filled in.

H J KINGSLEY (NORWICH) LTD

Kingsley House, Morris Street, Norwich NR6 7JM
Tel: (01603) 117097 Fax: (01603) 117099 Reg. No: England 12086215 VAT No: 8793519

Fax Message

To:
Name: Mr HT Taylor
Company: Health and Safety Executive
Fax No: 01353 112039

Message From: Tom Frost
Date: 16 March 1999

Please let us know by phone or fax immediately if any page is missing or garbled in transmission

Dear Mr Taylor,

We have just learned about the death of John Smith, a former employee, who was living at 34 Castle End, Midsham, Cambs and, in accordance with statutory requirements, we are writing to notify you of the fact.

We understand from his wife that his death was a direct result of an accident sustained while working here and which we notified you about on 30 October last year.

Yours sincerely

Mr Tom Frost
Health and Safety Officer

IDENDEN INDUSTRIES
A division of Idenden Plc
Porter House, Hull HU7 4RF England

Tel 01482 119087 Fax 01482 119088
Registered in England No: 1218943

3 December 1999

To all heads of department

Holidays
Until now, it has been a requirement of the company that everyone takes their holiday within one calendar year, and the right to any holiday not taken by the 31 December has lapsed.

It has now been decided to amend the rule, to give everyone the opportunity to be more flexible with their holidays. From today, anyone who has up to a week's holiday entitlement outstanding at the 31 December must use it up by 31 March in the following year. The entitlement to any days that are not used by the 31 March will lapse. Unused holiday may not be converted to pay. The entitlement to holiday is, of course, still subject to agreement with your manager. It must take into account the business and operational needs of the company and, especially, avoid clashes with other people; if this means that a job would be left uncovered.

If you have any queries about this new policy, please see Jemima Denoon.

Yours sincerely

A K Oakman
Personnel Executive

When changing the rules of the company, it is vital to be clear about what the changes mean for people and to set the boundaries of what is permitted.

Here, a fairly simple amendment gives rise to additional questions that the writer has tried to anticipate. Note how the letter begins with a statement of what the existing holiday policy is, so everyone is clear about how the changes differ.

┌─────────────────────┐
│ **CHAPTER FIVE** │
└─────────────────────┘

Sales and Marketing Management

Writing a really good sales letter that persuades customers to buy your product is one of the toughest assignments. You need to have an ear, not only for your product or service, but also for what makes your customers place their orders. Letters associated with other forms of selling are also depicted (for example, through agencies and distributors).

Letters that sell

Six letters that are designed to sell a product or service are given here (letters 71–6). Each one takes a slightly different standpoint and picks a different approach for getting through to the customer. You have to accept that you won't get through to everyone; it's all a question of which one produces the biggest response.

Letters to agents and distributors

Handling agents is a skill of its own and operating at a distance raises the importance of letters and faxes in maintaining the lines of communications. As letters 77–84 show, many different types have to be written to agents, from simple responses to motivational letters, reprimands and dismissals, each one requiring a different tone.

A letter that aims to sell the benefits of an organisation is not easy to make original. There are so many sales letters landing on people's desks that the potential buyer can quickly become immune to the messages being sent. Or they may feel that what is being said is just sales talk from the company, which may stop them responding.

This letter takes a different tack. Demonstrating that you have a host of satisfied customers proves more than simply saying 'our product is the best'. It is sufficient to make the reader sit up and think about what you are saying. At the very least, it gives him someone to contact to get a reference from. If you do use this approach, make sure you obtain the permission of the people mentioned in the letter.

Fenner & Sons

16 George Street, Woodbridge,
Suffolk IP3 7KL
Tel: (01394) 198423
Fax: (01394) 198444
Registered in England: 91221299
VAT No: 919129075 80

Mr J Jenkins
Training Manager
A M Clifton Ltd
18 Coltsfield
Royston
Herts
SG8 9LK

16 May 1999

Dear Mr Jenkins

Who are Fenner & Sons and why are we writing to you?

Fenner & Sons is a team of professional trainers, dedicated to helping management teams operate more effectively through tailor-made courses that enhance and perfect personal skills. Our courses really can help you:

- deliver professional presentations <u>every time</u>
- negotiate to win
- gain an extra ten hours a week.

But you don't have to take our word for it. Ask Janice Mitchell at BT, Kay Lewis at Smiths Accountants, John Allen at Anglian Water, Marcia Cavendish at Campbell and Young and Tim Free at Johnsons.

They all come to us regularly because <u>we give them exactly what they ask for</u>. Tailor-made training that develops the personal skills of their management teams – helping them to achieve what they want in their businesses.

Ask them about our understanding of these skills; our attention to detail; how we get the best out of you and, most importantly, the results in enhanced team performance. Janice Mitchell will be able to tell you <u>how she saved BT thousands of pounds</u> by using just one of the negotiating tactics she learned in the day.

And don't forget to ask them about the cost – I am sure you will then be convinced that our courses offer the most cost-effective way of training teams. If you are not entirely satisfied that the course was value for money we will even give you your money back. So what have you got to lose? Don't delay. For a confidential, no-commitment chat, call me now on 01394 198423.

Yours sincerely

Roger Harvey

PS. <u>Don't forget our money-back guarantee</u>. No other training company is willing to go this far to guarantee your satisfaction!

SIMPSON & MARTIN

39 TOP STREET
STOKE-ON-TRENT
ST2 3DR UNITED KINGDOM
Tel: (01782) 156232 Fax: (01782) 120899

Reg. No: England 96223978 VAT No: 91210674

1 July 1999

Dear Business Manager

The Insider Guide to Bank Lending
Just a quick note to let you know that "The Insider Guide to Bank Lending" has just arrived from the printers and it is so extraordinarily revealing that I felt I must personally urge you to take a look at it.

I wouldn't expect you or any senior manager to discuss your company's finances with people outside the organisation – but I defy anyone to look through "The Insider Guide to Bank Lending" and still be confident that they are getting the best deal from their bank. It reveals things non-bankers simply don't know about banks. It is bound to confirm some suspicions you have and it will blow away some seriously wrong assumptions.

But, critically, you can now see where and how you can negotiate down the costs, fees and charges we had all been encouraged to believe were written in stone.

It really is the most extraordinarily revealing guide to the way banks and bankers make lending decisions for business. I find the implications for the shift in negotiating power from the banks back to the customer very heartening indeed. For under £200, this heavyweight guide has the potential to save many businesses thousands. I am convinced it will be able to do the same for your business.

Incidentally, it also has over 400 pages of interest-rate tables and explanatory notes that make the guide, for me, utterly irresistible. The way the bank arrives at its figures has always been a frustrating mystery. Their numbers never seemed to quite tally with mine. There is only so much time and energy you can give when the individual instances are not that large. But they do mount up.

The interest-rate tables explain exactly what is going on and, for the first time, you can now quickly and confidently check and challenge the bank's figures. You might also discover some instances where you just could be better off on a different type of loan.

I have enclosed a copy of the brochure we are preparing for "The Insider Guide to Bank Lending". Do have a look at it – I am sure you will see why I am so enthusiastic about this book and why I felt it was important to write to you immediately about it.

Yours sincerely.

Andrew Clifford
Marketing Manager

PS Although the enclosed brochure is still our working draft, please feel free to use it to order your copy.
16 June 1999

This letter uses the sense that you are being let in on a secret here, something that is new and incredible. This sense of curiosity is built up by "Just a quick note to let you know...". Having it come from an enthusiastic devotee of the product, rather than the publisher, gives the endorsement greater weight and credibility in the eyes of the reader. Note how this personal enthusiasm is sustained in phrases such as "...that make the guide, for me, utterly irresistible".

There is also a nice grouping of words that add power and persuasion in phrases like: "...quickly and confidently check and challenge...". The persuasive manner is sustained to the end with the urgent "Do have a look at it...". A subtle touch is deployed in the PS: calling the brochure a 'working draft' adds to the sense of immediacy and urgency, by implying that the writer couldn't wait to let you know about the new book.

Customers can fall away for many reasons and it is not always easy to tell why. Sometimes, it may simply be that they have forgotten about you. It is certainly easier to try and revive lapsed customers than it is to find new ones. You have one big advantage with a lapsed customer – they already know you and so you don't have to waste time explaining who you are and what you are offering.

Here, a service has been improved and the aim is to attract back customers to try out the revised version to see if it meets their needs. Note the tactic used to make the customer feel he is receiving special treatment: "I've set aside some copies...", giving the impression that some have been specially reserved. And the tactic used to obtain a rapid response in the penultimate paragraph, which seeks action: "Just complete the fax-back acceptance offer...before everyone else does".

SIMPSON & MARTIN

39 TOP STREET
STOKE-ON-TRENT
ST2 3DR UNITED KINGDOM
Tel: (01782) 156232 Fax: (01782) 120899
Reg. No: England 96223978 VAT No: 91210674

Dear Customer

I've set aside some copies of the July issue of Book-Talk to give away on a 'first come, first served' basis to past subscribers who haven't yet tried the NEW Book-Talk . I want you to be able to judge for yourself – **absolutely free**.

You'll really appreciate the differences we've made – Book-Talk now gives you far more of the essence of the books reviewed than ever before – and it is now produced in the UK under our direct control, using professional broadcasters and quality-sound reproduction techniques.

The July issue features the latest book by *Will Carling and Robert Heller – The Way to Win*. It's only been published for a couple of months now and has already become a best-seller through the book trade – and no wonder! It's a fascinating book, an extraordinary meeting of minds between two leaders in the fields of sporting and business leadership. Together they explain the motivational techniques that can be used to generate success in business – they're practical, usable ideas you can use right now in your job or business.

While stocks last, I would be happy to send you the July issue <u>absolutely free</u>.

This special offer is strictly on a first come, first served basis. (One of the advantages of Electronic Post is that everyone gets their letter on the same day.) But there is no obligation. You get the tapes. You can listen to them. You can decide whether to continue your subscription or cancel it. You keep the July issue either way.

I KNOW that once you've heard the new Book-Talk for yourself you will be convinced that it is what you need – to save you time, to make good use of that otherwise wasted time in the car, to keep you ahead of the latest business thinking and practice every month. So take me up on my offer and try it!

So – what do you do next? Just complete the fax-back acceptance offer overleaf and fax it back to us on 01782 120899 – before everyone else does. Or phone, quoting ref TB6, or post it to us in the reply-paid envelope supplied.

I look forward to hearing from you. I'm confident you will be impressed with the new Book-Talk.

Yours sincerely

Andrew Clifford
Marketing Manager

Save the Kids in Rio Mission

114 St Vincents Street, LONDON N3 9GH England
Tel: (0171) 115 1280 Fax: (0171) 115 1811

Registered Charity No: 4577606

Mr J Garfield
Hill Rise
High Street
Milton Keynes
MK12 7HY

15 April 1999

Dear Mr Garfield

Three years ago Pablo, a nine-year-old child, was left on the streets of Rio to die. He was turned out by his parents, who were too poor to look after him. For over a year, he managed to eke out a living by begging on the streets. But it was no life – every day was a nightmare of survival – just to get enough to eat. With nowhere to live and nowhere to sleep it could hardly get worse. Except for Pablo it did.

One day, Pablo found himself 'in the way' of a group of other boys, scarcely older than himself, who decided that he was 'on their patch'. A fight ensued in which Pablo received several stab wounds from a six-inch blade and was left to die in a gutter. Pablo had done no wrong. He had committed no crime. His only fault was to be in the wrong place at the wrong time. Luckily for Pablo, a helper from the Save the Kids in Rio Mission was walking along the street seconds after the attack happened. Without this miracle of timing, Pablo would now be dead.

Today, thanks to the Save the Kids in Rio Mission, Pablo has recovered from his wounds. And although his life is still no bed of roses, he does at least receive enough to eat, he has a place to sleep safely and he has started to learn to read and write.

The sad fact is that every year hundreds of kids like Pablo are needlessly dying on the streets of Rio. But the good news is that the Save the Kids in Rio Mission are doing just that – <u>saving them</u>. We can't cure the problem, but we can go a little way to help and that is what we are asking you to do. Not to cure the problem <u>but to go just a little way to help the hundreds of kids like Pablo that we manage to save each year</u>.

I hope that you will be able to find the heart to help Pablo – <u>£15 will provide Pablo and others like him with enough food for two months</u>. It's not a lot to ask. Of course, if you would like to sponsor a child under the Save the Kids in Rio scheme, then we can send you a full information pack, telling you how you can save a life. Just tick the box on the enclosed reply-paid envelope and send it back to us.

Yours sincerely

H A Hart
Appeals Manager

PS Remember, £15 is all it takes to feed Pablo for two months.

Capturing attention is one of the main ingredients of success with sales letters. Everyone likes a story – particularly one that arouses your curiosity and makes you want to read on. It is, therefore, a style that fits naturally with letters that sell.

Here, a semi-tragic story is used to arouse emotional feelings in the reader that will make him or her respond with a donation to the charity. The appealing to emotion is sustained with phrases like: "...go a little way to help..."; "...find the heart to help..." and "It's not a lot to ask...".

If customers are subscribing to a service, at some point they may actively have to renew their subscriptions.

Never take it for granted that they will continue. Instead, treat a renewal letter as an opportunity to remind them of the benefits they are receiving from their subscription and to sell the idea to them again. If they are undecided whether to renew, it could be enough to tip the balance in your favour.

Here, incentives of lower subscriptions and the chance to win a free safari are used to sustain subscribers' interests.

Wildlife Today

11 Courtney Way, Evesham, Worcestershire WR11 3RF

Registered in England No: 39789622 VAT No: 911674210

Mr M Little
1 Chelmwood Road
Lincoln
LN6 7JU

7 May 1999

Dear Mr Little,

Your subscription to Wildlife Today will be expiring within the next three months.

I am sure that you wish to avoid the irritation of an interrupted delivery and the inconvenience of missed issues. To help us avoid this, please return the attached Renewal Invoice, together with your cheque or credit card authorisation, as soon as possible.

This may seem excessively early to remind you, but it helps us to keep your issues flowing. The sooner we receive your renewal, the sooner you can rest assured your magazines will keep coming.

Remember, subscribing for three years will save you a staggering 50% off the cover price, 45% off two years and 40% for one year. Now, isn't that unbeatable value?

You can also have the chance to win a free safari to Kenya. To take advantage of this opportunity, all you need to do is to complete the enclosed questionnaire, which is designed to tell us what you think about Wildlife Today, and return it with your renewal payment advice.

Yours sincerely

D A Cross
Editor

PS Don't forget to enclose the customer questionnaire with your payment advice. Without it you will not be eligible for our free prize draw to win a safari to Kenya.

Kelso Limited
16 Abbots Road, Luton, Bedford MK44 7YT
Tel: (01234) 136953 Fax: (01234) 136422
Registered in England No: 9126719 VAT No: 91523489 76

Mr T Collins
J T Cunningham & Co
74 Bridgend
Maidstone
Kent

17 April 1999

Dear Tony,

It was a pleasure to meet you yesterday, especially as our only previous contact was a dim and distant conversation by 'phone.

I confirm that we would be delighted to help with your computing needs, when the time is right for you. As promised, I enclose a summary of the computing services we can offer, which have been created and driven entirely by the needs of our customers.

The situation you described, and your experiences with mainframe computing, have a familiar ring. Your ideas on the PC approach would be well worth pursuing and I am certain we would be able to give you access to your data in the way you want, either on an interim or a long-term basis.

As I mentioned, William Smith is our computer specialist and he would be very happy to look at the situation with you in due course, to see what might be done.

In the meantime, if you have any queries, please give me a ring.

Best wishes

Colin Frost
Sales Manager

Meetings present good opportunities to develop contacts and demonstrate the services that you can offer. Their difficulty is that they tend to be ephemeral and quickly forgotten.

Follow up with a letter, though, and you are doubling your impact on the person you met, giving a more lasting way of remembering you. It also demonstrates your professionalism and interest in him.

You won't get results from this type of letter all the time but, from the ones that you do, it could well have been the follow-up letter that made all the difference.

Obtaining representation of a company's products is a highly competitive business. It is a relatively easy field to enter so there can be many players in a market. The one factor that people will be looking out for, though, is performance. If you can demonstrate your advantage and success, you should at least get the opportunity to make a presentation to a business.

This letter uses a combination of gentle flattery: "...I am very impressed by their versatility..." and a clear demonstration of results "...<u>In the last three years we have increased the value of our sales into Europe by over 150%</u>". The overall tone is one of crisp professionalism and would certainly help to open many doors.

Thomas King & Palmer Ltd

serving the world

24 Fuller Road, Welling,
Kent DA16 7JP
Tel : (01322) 100132
Fax : (01322) 100178

Reg. No : England 1212298762
VAT No : 92905643

Mr P George
Marketing Manager
Norton & Brand Ltd
Hall Farm Ind Est
Wallington
Surrey
SM6 7HJ

16 July 1999

Dear Mr George,

I recently saw details of your company's range of conference, presentation and planning products. I am very impressed by their versatility, design and practicality.

We act as European agents for a select number of companies that produce presentation equipment. Instead of selling through stationers and office suppliers, we sell products direct to the end user. Our customers are large and medium-sized companies throughout mainland Europe. <u>In the last three years we have increased the value of our sales in Europe by over 150%.</u>

Over 1000 major European companies do business with us every year and our team of representatives visits each of them regularly. The secret to our rapid increase in sales is that we offer a faster supply and more personal service than our competitors. This simple formula, combined with the professionalism of our representatives, has made us the leading agent in the mainland European market.

I would like to discuss acting for you in this market and hope you can agree to an early meeting. I can be contacted on 01322 100132.

I look forward to hearing from you.

Yours sincerely

Helen Bye
European Sales Manager

RPP Holdings Plc
35/38 New Road, Paignton, Devon TQ3 4UU
Tel: 01803 175653 Fax: 01803 187908
Reg. No: England 1976143

Mr T G Smith,
22 Rue De La Cambre
B2100 Brussels
Belgium

26 June 1999

Dear Mr Smith,

Further to my letter of 13 June and our telephone conversation about your becoming a European agent for RRP, I have the following suggestion to make.

We have discussed this in some detail and, while we are keen to create new opportunities for our products in international markets, we have decided that we do not have the resources to give our customers a level of service that they need and expect. The delays which would inevitably occur in supplying individual customers on the continent from the UK, combined with the additional costs of delivering single orders, does not make it feasible for us to contemplate a commission-only agency.

I wonder if you might be interested in becoming a distributor for us instead? It seems that, if you are already handling the distribution for Hermann's, our product range would complement it well. We would be prepared to supply the range to you on consignment, rather than asking you to purchase the goods on your account, which would reduce the risk for you.

Please let me know if this arrangement is of interest to you and perhaps we can then meet to discuss the details further.

Yours sincerely

P F Davis
Director

The supplying company for whom Mr Smith is planning to act wants to try and persuade him not to take up an agency status (supplying orders and earning commission) but to become a distributor, who would take stock on a consignment basis to sell.

Note how the supplying company tries to persuade Mr Smith to accept this offer. It is phrased initially as a gentle suggestion : "I wonder if you might be interested in becoming...". Their proposal is supported by a reasonable and logical argument: "It seems that, if you are already handling the distribution for Hermann's, our product range would complement it well".

The supplier then appears to deal with one of the main objections that Mr Smith might raise: "We would be prepared to supply the range to you on consignment...". The reader is gently persuaded to consider the offer.

Increasing the capacity of agents to earn more is a big motivating factor for them. Recognition plays a part too, and this letter combines both elements.

The agent of the year award provides recognition, but recognition is given in the letter as well: " I am confident it is going to give us our best year ever. Your role in this, is, of course, pivotal. In recognition of this...". The prospect of a hefty bonus if a target is met gives the monetary incentive to perform.

Fenner & Sons

16 George Street, Woodbridge,
Suffolk IP3 7KL
Tel: (01394) 198423
Fax: (01394) 198444
Registered in England: 91221299
VAT No: 919129075 80

Craig Scott
P C Wright Ltd
4 Nightingale Way
Skipton
North Yorkshire

19 December 1999

Dear Craig,

Congratulations. You came very close to achieving our agent of the year award for an outstanding performance but John Wills in the south-west pipped you to the post. I wish you every success in achieving this accolade next year.

In the last twelve months, you have achieved 1200 unit sales with a total value of £600,000. As the latest edition of our catalogue shows, we have an excellent range of new products for this forthcoming year. I am confident it is going to give us our best year ever. Your role in this, is, of course, pivotal. In recognition of this, I would like to readjust our terms with you. You are currently receiving a flat 8% commission on all sales achieved in your territory. I would like to maintain that flat rate with you but if you achieve £750,000 sales value or more within the twelve months commencing 1 January, we shall award you a bonus of 2% on the value of all sales achieved within the year. The bonus shall be payable one month after the end of the calendar year. However, if the value of sales does not reach £750,000, the bonus will not be payable.

I hope you have a very successful and prosperous New Year.

Yours sincerely

Mark Turner
Sales Director

IDENDEN INDUSTRIES
A division of Idenden Plc
Porter House, Hull HU7 4RF England

Tel 01482 119087 Fax 01482 119088
Registered in England No: 1218943

Pierre Balan
Director General
Roodebeek Associates
Ev Swedenlann 7
B-2100 Brussels
Belgium

11 November 1999

Dear Pierre,

Re: Hugh Murphy Limited
It has come to my attention that you are acting as an agent for one of our competitors, Hugh Murphy Limited.

As you know, the terms of our agreement expressly forbid you either to act for any of our competitors or promote or sell any product or item which may be construed by us as competing with our products. Although we have every right to cancel your agreement, because of your exemplary performance to date, we are prepared to give you a second chance. I would, though, like your written assurance that you will not in future act for this or any other competitor of ours. If you are in any doubt about whether a company is a competitor or not, would you please discuss the matter with me personally.

If you feel that you are unable to generate sufficient business from our range of products or to give the assurance requested then we shall have no option but to cancel our agreement and look for an alternative agent.

I look forward to hearing from you.

Yours sincerely

Bill Tanner
European Marketing Director

This letter is threatening strong action to be taken unless the agent ceases to act for a competitor.

The company would be within their rights to terminate the agreement immediately. However, they are prepared to give the agent a second chance because of the "...exemplary performance..." which he has shown.

Note the opening which doesn't declare how the news reached him (something that the agent will be curious to know) but just states, quite simply: "It has come to my attention...".

Dismissing an agent who has breached a contract requires a little thought. You need to make sure that you are acting completely within your rights, in case the agent decides to bring an action for damages against you.

This letter records the story word for word, making sure that the steps that have been taken can be defended, even if the agent decided to bring legal action. Note how the letter mentions the meeting at which he was "...unable to give us a satisfactory reason..." why he had been working for a competitor. The fact there has been "...previous misconduct..." will also support the claim.

This letter should deter the agent from bringing an action against the company for wrongful dismissal (if he was considering it) as well as act as a record of what happened.

IDENDEN INDUSTRIES
A division of Idenden Plc
Porter House, Hull HU7 4RF England

Tel 01482 119087 Fax 01482 119088
Registered in England No: 1218943

Pierre Balan
Director General
Roodebeek Associates
Ev Swedenlann 7
B-2100 Brussels
Belgium

20 December 1999

Dear Pierre,

Re: Johnson Murray Ltd

It has been brought to my attention that once again you are acting for a competitor of ours, in direct contravention of our agreement.

At our meeting today, you were unable to give us a satisfactory reason why you have been acting for Johnson Murray Ltd at the same time as for ourselves. I would also like to remind you that, on 12 November, you admitted to having worked for Hugh Murphy Ltd at the same time as for us. In your letter of 13 November, you gave us your written assurances that you would not act for any competitor, under any circumstances, while you were acting as our agent.

In view of your previous misconduct, and clause 6b of our agreement, which forbids you to act for any of our competitors, I regard this as a serious breach of our contract and have no alternative but to cancel our agreement with immediate effect.

Yours sincerely

Bill Tanner
European Marketing Director

Hart & Tucker Ltd

19 Green Street, Maidstone, Kent ME41 1TJ
Telephone: (01622) 109109
Facsimile: (01622) 108106
Reg. No: England 96223978 VAT No: 91210674

Brian Henderson
Marketing Director
B & R Hendersons Ltd
Marlows Road
Aberdeen
AB20 5GT

30 June 1999

Dear Brian,

We have been reviewing our commission structure and, in particular, the relationship between the cost of making sales to the amount we receive from you.

Since we took over this agency five years ago, sales of your products in our territory have risen from £250,000 to £650,000 a year. In that time, the activities that we have been compelled to make to obtain the increase have risen out of all proportion. We now hold the view that unless we are able to agree an increase in commission (only by a modest 5 per cent), we shall not be able to sustain the growth rates that have been achieved formerly.

I hope that you are able to agree to this small contribution towards our continued mutual success, and look forward to receiving your reply.

Yours sincerely

Barry Hall
Marketing Manager

Putting in a claim for a higher payment or commission always requires careful thought. It will inevitably be met by a wall of resistance from the other side, as no one wishes to have their margins affected.

Note the arguments that the company has to consider. The agency has obtained a strong sales growth for the company. It has cost the agent a lot to achieve those sales - costs that the agency, not the company, has borne. What the agency is banking on, to make their negotiations succeed, is the success that they have enjoyed in obtaining a strong sales growth. It therefore does not seem unreasonable to request an increase in commission "...by a modest 5 per cent...", which the agent understates by calling it a "...small contribution towards our continued mutual success...".

If the company refuses to increase the agent's commission, it will demoralise them. The agency is clearly successful and this success increases its negotiating power. If the company accepts the agency's demand, its margins will be affected.

Instead, the company finds a lateral solution. It cleverly latches on to the point made by the agency when it said "...we shall not be able to sustain the growth rates that have been achieved formerly". The company's counter proposal, therefore, links an increase in performance to an increase in commission in that the increase will have to "...be earned through additional sales...". This way, no one is the loser and everyone has the potential to earn more.

B & R HENDERSONS LTD

Marlows Road, Aberdeen AB20 5GT
Tel: 01224 267855 Fax: 01224 267977
Reg. No: 16497811 VAT No: 7387945

Barry Hall
Marketing Manager
Hart & Tucker Ltd
19 Green Street
Maidstone
Kent
ME41 1TJ

15 July 1999

Dear Barry,

Thank you for your letter of 30 June, requesting an increase in your commission from 10% this year to 15% next year on all the sales you make.

While I wish that we could say a straight 'yes', we could not accept a reduction in our margins without any guarantee of a return. Any increase that we give in commission will have to be earned through additional sales. As an incentive, if you achieve £750,000 sales value or more within the next twelve months we are prepared to award you a bonus of 2% on the value of all sales achieved within the year. The bonus would be payable one month after the end of the calendar year but would be subject to the threshold of £750,000 being achieved within the year.

I hope this proposal might be of interest to you and look forward to hearing from you.

Yours sincerely

Brian Henderson
Marketing Director

IDENDEN INDUSTRIES
A division of Idenden Plc
Porter House, Hull HU7 4RF England

Tel 01482 119087 Fax 01482 119088
Registered in England No: 1218943

Mr D Basantani
Director
Teban Kian Pte Ltd
Blk 31 Heng Gardens Road
Tampines Industrial Park
5100 Kuala Lumpur
Malaysia

1 October 1999

Dear Mr Basantani,

Notice of Proposed Surcharge
As you are no doubt aware, recent events in the financial market have put intense pressure on sterling, which has lost considerable ground against most major currencies. The majority of products we sell are paid for in Dutch guilders, and the effect on our transactions has been considerable.

We recognise that turbulent exchange-rate fluctuations could mean that the current situation improves, and, therefore, we will refrain from implementing a surcharge immediately.

If, however, the situation does not improve by the end of October, we will be forced to implement a surcharge on all orders received after the 30th October 1999.

I sincerely hope we shall not have to resort to this action, but trust you appreciate its necessity should the situation not improve.

Yours sincerely,

John Black
International Marketing Manager

Agents and distributors can take a lot of managing. If you can avoid it, try not to spring nasty surprises on them – give them ample warning about changes to prices or commission.

Issuing an advance warning gives the agent the chance to get used to the idea before it is implemented. It will be a lot easier for him to swallow and will be less likely to cause bad feeling, in what is often a delicate relationship that relies on goodwill from both sides.

Here, the company is issuing a warning that a surcharge may become necessary. The circumstances are outside their control as it is due to exchange-rate fluctuations. Setting a clear timetable for action puts everyone clearly in the picture and will be a lot easier for the distributor to accept than if it was suddenly sprung upon him.

CHAPTER SIX

Banking, Insurance and Property

This chapter focuses on letters that are ancillary to many core business activities but which are no less important to the smooth running of a business. Everything from dealing with an estate agent, insurance broker and bank is considered. Indeed, if a business does not enjoy good relations with its bank, it may find it hard to survive at all.

Banking letters
The routine letters to a bank illustrate opening an account, closing an account and declining an offer to open an account.

Insurance
The letters here deal with requests for insurance and for a revised quotation.

Property
When making offers to estate agents it is important to confirm what is included, to avoid misunderstandings at a later stage. The letters here show how to handle it.

When opening a current account, a bank will need to know some basic information before it accepts you as a customer. The customer here is already known to the bank, so it is able to dispense with the usual formalities. Don't forget a bank will want to know who the signatories to an account will be, whether the account is 'both to sign' or 'either to sign' and what name the account should be in.

PARKER
Glass Ltd

Unit 27 Willow Park
Christchurch, Dorset BH23 6MM
Tel: 01202 109111
Fax: 01202 109112

Reg. No: England 962578762
VAT No: 9120564

Mr F Turner
Manager
RSH Bank Plc
73 Main Street
Dorset
BH23 6MM

3 May 1999

Dear Mr Turner,

We are reorganising the administration of our accounts department and wish to open another current account, from which all our suppliers will be paid. Our existing current account No. 629523 will be used for all other transactions.

I would be grateful if you could arrange for £10,000 to be transferred from Account No. 629523 to the new account. The signatories for the new account will be myself and Mary Martin. You already have my specimen signature on file and I enclose a sample of Mary Martin's signature. Both signatures will be required on all cheques. The account should be in the name Parker Enterprises.

I look forward to receiving a chequebook for the new account.

Yours sincerely

A Parker
Finance Director

Tyler & Piper Associates

76 Whites Lane, Stevenage, Herts SG1 8JP England
Tel: (01438) 186465 Fax: (01438) 164323

Mr K Foster
Manager
Martins Bank PLC
54 High Street
Stevenage
Herts
SG1 8JP

17 April 1999

Dear Mr Foster,

Account no. 354896
We no longer need our account no. 354896 and I would be grateful if it
could be closed immediately.

Please transfer the remaining balance to account no. 729491.

Yours sincerely

S R Piper
Finance Manager/Partner

Partners: DA Tyler BA & SR Piper MA

Banks will usually require instructions about closing accounts to be made in writing. A simple letter like this one is all that is required. Don't forget to include details of where you want the remaining balance of the account to go to.

A company has been offered terms to open an account, but it has decided to shop around for a better rate. A bank will always appreciate knowing why you are not opening an account. Don't forget to keep your letter courteous – you never know when you may need the services of that bank again in the future.

Grange & Turner Ltd

32 WESTBOURN ROAD, WITNEY, OXON OX6 7HY

Telephone (01993) 107888
Fax (01993) 107843

Reg. No: England 13078453
VAT No: 75698764

Mrs Y Norman
Business Manager
Barkers Bank plc
23 High Street
Witney
Oxon
OX6 7HY

20 June 1999

Dear Mrs Norman

Thank you for your letter of 12 June, outlining the terms on which you are willing to provide us with an overdraft and current account.

We have considered your offer but regret that we shall not be opening an account with you, as we have been able to secure an overdraft rate with Macaulays Bank which is 0.5% lower.

Thank you for your time considering our application and I hope we may have an opportunity to do business in future.

Yours sincerely

DG Edwards
Director

Fenner & Sons

16 George Street, Woodbridge,
Suffolk IP3 7KL
Tel: (01394) 198423
Fax: (01394) 198444
Registered in England: 91221299
VAT No: 919129075 80

Mr Kevin Little
Barker Insurance Brokers
24 Middle Street
Ipswich
IP2 3TY

20 March 1999

Dear Kevin,

Re: Buildings Insurance for 45 Edmunds Street, Bury
We are about to acquired a detached property at 45 Edmunds Street,
Bury which we shall be using as commercial premises. We anticipate
signing the purchase contract towards the end of next month.

The premises will not be occupied for two months, so we are concerned
to insure the building only at this stage. I enclose a copy of the
valuation report on the building, which estimates the rebuilding cost at
£105,000.

We would like to effect an all-risks policy and I would be grateful if you
could let me have your quotation for the most favourable rates.

Yours sincerely

George Rose
Director

Insurance on property
should be effected from
the moment that you
become responsible for
it, not from the date of
occupation.

This letter requests a
company to arrange
insurance cover for a
building that has just
been purchased. To
insure the building, the
insurer needs to know
the address of the
property, the date from
when insurance needs to
take effect, the value of
the property (which the
building valuation report
will provide) and the
type of policy required.

It is important that life insurance and pension arrangements are reviewed periodically. If there are discrepancies between policies, make sure these are investigated adequately. This letter is asking for revised quotations to vary the benefits.

Taylor Taylor & Shaw

Benton House, Clifton, Bristol BS16 7LJ
Tel: (0117) 1089254   Fax: (0117) 1089211

Mr. R Denny
Shipleys Insurance Brokers
11 Wallace Road
Bristol
BS4 5FD

14 March 1999

Dear Bob,

Re: Pension scheme
I have just been reviewing our pension scheme and my wife is concerned that her scheme does not appear to have a 'death in service' benefit, although mine does. Please advise what the additional cost of this benefit would be.

I am also considering increasing the life assurance that is attached to my pension, from £150,000 to £250,000. Please also advise me what difference this would make to the monthly premium.

Yours sincerely,

A W Taylor

Partners: AW Taylor & GS Taylor

Thomas King & Palmer Ltd
serving the world

24 Fuller Road, Welling,
Kent DA16 7JP
Tel : (01322) 100132
Fax : (01322) 100178

Reg. No : England 1212298762
VAT No : 92905643

Mr Eddie Wright
Hope Taylor & Moore
35 Lion Row
Dartford
Kent
DA3 2ON

14 May 1999

Subject to Contract

Dear Mr Wright,

12a High Street, Welling
Further to our telephone conversation this morning, I am writing to confirm our offer of £76,000 to purchase the above property.

This offer is to include all carpets, blinds, fixtures and fittings at the premises.

Yours sincerely

F G York
Director

If you make an offer on a property, the estate agent will confirm it with you in writing. It is advisable that you also confirm the price that has been agreed and any other items that are to be included in the sale, such as carpets and blinds.

It is easy for misunderstandings to occur over the telephone and, if the agent has it in writing from you, it will save arguments later on.

Heading your letter 'Subject to contract' under English law does not bind you to the sale until contracts have been signed and exchanged.

If you decide to make an offer that is subject to certain conditions, it is important that you spell out exactly what those conditions are. This letter is applying pressure on the sellers to move out sooner than they initially wanted and to have a local authority easement (right of access over the property) released.

The penultimate paragraph (notifying the agent about instructing a solicitor and arranging for a valuation) is designed to convey confidence to the agent and seller about your seriousness in going through with the sale.

H J KINGSLEY (NORWICH) LTD

Kingsley House, Morris Street, Norwich NR6 7JM
Tel: (01603) 117097 Fax: (01603) 117099 Reg. No: England 12086215 VAT No: 8793519

Mr S Clark
Foster & Clark
56 Baker Street
Norwich
NR3 1QA

20 April 1999

Subject to Contract

Dear Simon

15 Forest Row, Norwich

Just to confirm our discussion today.

We undertake to increase our offer from £120,000 to £125,000 for the purchase of 15 Forest Row, Norwich. This additional sum is offered on the basis that The Stone Partnership undertake to have the local authority easement released, prior to exchange of contracts. Any costs relating to having the easement released shall be the responsibility of The Stone Partnership. We do not wish to delay completion until mid-July as suggested to you by Mr Jones of the Stone Partnership (for which the lesser sum of £120,000 would have been payable). This additional sum of £5000 is also being offered on the basis that The Stone Partnership aim to exchange contracts with us at the earliest practicable date, which we anticipate being in the week beginning 17 April, with completion occurring 3 weeks later, in the week beginning 8 May.

I understand that The Stone Partnership has accepted this arrangement and these time scales should be realistic, allowing sufficient time for all the paperwork to be completed and for the easement to be released. I have, therefore, instructed our solicitor to continue with the sale and am making arrangements for the valuation on the property to be carried out.

I trust this is a satisfactory summary of our conversation and that the sale will proceed smoothly.

Yours sincerely,

Peter Hills
Director

CHAPTER SEVEN

International Trade

International trade transactions are notoriously complex and require specialist knowledge, to ensure that the hurdles are straddled successfully. The letters in this chapter aim to give a flavour of the correspondence that is needed in these transactions, although you must bear in mind that individual circumstances will vary for each separate transaction that is carried out. Nevertheless, the hints and tips are sufficient to give a clear idea about how to set out correspondence and the kind of transactions that you can expect to have to deal with.

Quotations and orders
When making quotes and setting down payment terms, a greater precision is required than with goods sold domestically. You need to be sure the recipient is clear exactly what is included and how far a product is to be delivered within the charges set out.

How are the goods to be paid for?
Pressing a debtor to pay in a foreign country is likely to be difficult, if the customer defaults on payment. It is far better to make sure that payment is secure before the goods are despatched. Letter 94 deals with asking a bank to pay on the presentation of a letter of credit.

Transporting the goods
You are reasonably sure that you will be paid for your exports but a lot can happen to the goods, between their leaving your premises and arriving at their destination. To minimise the problems the packing list details need to be correct and confirmed with the customer as in letter 95.

This letter is to a potential new client. With international clients, you need to be more careful about payment terms. Here, the supplier is indicating that payment must be by a guaranteed method, such as an Irrevocable Letter of Credit, which is a written undertaking between the buyer's bank and the exporter to pay. The documents and conditions must be precisely in order. The smallest mistake can delay payment.

Thomas King & Palmer Ltd

serving the world

24 Fuller Road, Welling,
Kent DA16 7JP
Tel : (01322) 100132
Fax : (01322) 100178

Reg. No : England 1212298762
VAT No : 92905643

N Kiyeyo (Graphic Arts) Limited
Kiyeyo House
10 Santa Maria Street
Valletta
Malta

25 August 1999

Dear Sirs,

Many thanks for your fax of 21st August and your interest in our products.

I have pleasure in enclosing two copies of our brochure, outlining our main products. As you can appreciate, the diversity of requirements in the printing and graphic arts industries precludes us from listing all of the available items. We would, of course, be very pleased to quote and supply against specific requests.

Our terms of payment are normally Irrevocable Letter of Credit, confirmed on a prime U.K. bank or pre-payment in pounds sterling. However, we have learned that our own bankers, the Cooperative Bank plc, are a correspondent bank to the Bank of Valletta and we would, therefore, accept a 30-day bank draft or faxed guarantee of payment bank-to-bank.

We are solely an export company and, therefore, you can feel confident in our ability to deal with shipping, export packing and documentation. We are also aware of the special requirements of hot and/or dusty environments and many of our products are specifically formulated to cope with these conditions.

I would like you to thank Mr. Bernard Thomas for his prompt introduction and I very much look forward to dealing with you in the future.

Yours faithfully,

Helen Smith
International Sales

IDENDEN INDUSTRIES
A division of Idenden Plc
Porter House, Hull HU7 4RF England

Tel 01482 119087 Fax 01482 119088
Registered in England No: 1218943

Mr Hailu Indieka
Director
IMTU
PO Box 1120
Addis Ababa
Ethiopia

28 February 1999

Dear Mr Indieka,

Pro forma Nos 11938665 and 11938667
Many thanks for your letter of 16 February.

I enclose pro formas for the KORD 64 machines which we currently have on our books. I would like to advise you that, upon receipt of your letter of credit for whichever machine you think is preferable, our engineers will commence work in stripping down and re-furbishing. This work will take approximately three weeks.

I trust that you find our offers of interest and look forward to receiving your letter of credit shortly.

Yours sincerely,

John Foster
International Sales

A buyer is interested in purchasing some reconditioned machines. The supplier will only agree to sell them, provided that payment is made by a documentary letter of credit. The supplier starts the ball rolling by issuing a pro forma invoice requesting payment by letter of credit. Until the letter of credit is in place, the supplying company will not commence work on the goods, giving the buyer an incentive to complete the paperwork quickly.

Before a bank will pay out against an irrevocable letter of credit, it will demand that all the documentation is correct. The exact documentation required will vary depending on the countries the goods are going to and from.

Setting the documents out as a list will help you to check that nothing has been omitted and enable the bank to check more easily that they have received all the items that you declare are enclosed.

IDENDEN INDUSTRIES
A division of Idenden Plc
Porter House, Hull HU7 4RF England

Tel 01482 119087 Fax 01482 119088

Registered in England No: 1218943

A & A Bank
Bills and Credits Department
Mint House
PO Box 10
Monting Court
London WE1 9DP

Dear Sirs,

Your Ref: E54000/1002

Re: Irrevocable Documentary Credit No: 92000026 for $21,640.00
From: Bank of Ghana Limited, Accra
Consignee: Hellpack Industries Limited, Accra

With regard to the above, we enclose your original credit documents, together with the following:-

1. 3 copies original certificate of Value
2. 3 copies commercial invoice
3. Full set less 1 original plus 2 non-negotiable copies of bill of lading.
4. Original clean report of findings plus embossed and signed invoice
5. 2 copies packing list
6. Our certification that we have sent the appropriate copies of the documents to the opener
7. Our draft to the value of $17,800.00
8. 2 copies certificate of analysis

I trust that everything is in order and we would ask you to pay this directly to our account as follows and notify us accordingly:-

Barkers Bank PLC
Overseas Financial Services
10 Blair Street
London E1 8BL

Account Name: Idenden Industries
Account No: 3156974582

Many thanks for your co-operation.

Yours faithfully,

John Foster
International Sales

IDENDEN INDUSTRIES
A division of Idenden Plc
Porter House, Hull HU7 4RF England

Tel 01482 119087 Fax 01482 119088
Registered in England No: 1218943

Mr A Ngwako
Mellpack Industries Limited
PO Box 1121
Addis Ababa
Ethiopia

23 April 1999

Dear Abraham,

IDR No: RID 92 203425/001

I confirm that the packing-list details, which we sent to you on 10 April, contained the following information:

Shipped on Board Vessel Veronique Delmas 9th April 1999
BOL No. 4014 - Container No. PACG 000761-0

1 x 20ft container containing:

80 drums of 180kg each net (14,400kg) Ethyl Acetate

Gross weight per drum - 197.50kg   Tare 17.5kg

TOTAL WEIGHT - 15,800KG   GROSS TARE - 1,400KG

MARKS: Mellpack
          Addis Ababa
          Ethiopia

Ethyl Acetate
U.N. No 1956

Yours sincerely

David Wilson
International Sales Manager

A packing list has gone astray and a client has asked for a confirmation of what it contained.

The 'tare' is the weight of the container in which the goods are carried (without the goods).

The marks identify how the container has been labelled for shipping purposes, to help with identification.

The pre-shipment inspection agency requires a packing list, showing the items that are to be inspected. A danger with this procedure is that inspection will not have occurred before they are due to be shipped. Specifying when you want the goods to be inspected, together with details of the shipping date, enables the inspection company to plan in good time.

IDENDEN INDUSTRIES
A division of Idenden Plc
Porter House, Hull HU7 4RF England

Tel 01482 119087 Fax 01482 119088
Registered in England No: 1218943

Bureau Veritas
Westdlaak 5 - 9 3012KC
PO Box 2705
3000 CS Rotterdam
The Netherlands

2 April 1999

Dear Sirs,

Re: IDR: RTD 92 203425/001
92 - MD793848
BA-920123-036
MELLPACK INDUSTRIES ETHIOPIA

With reference to the above, I enclose two copies of the packing list. I trust this will assist your inspector.

As previously stated, we are looking forward to inspection in the week commencing 23rd March, to enable us to ship on a vessel loading on 27th March.

Many thanks for your co-operation.

Yours faithfully,

Claire Scott
International Sales

CHAPTER EIGHT

Business and the Community

All businesses will, to some extent, have dealings with the community in which they are involved. The letters in this chapter deal with requests for charitable donations, invitations to speak at meetings and local planning issues.

Requests and invitations
Handling requests from charities for donations that you are going to accept is easier than declining requests. You have to counter the impression of being mean-minded and uncharitable and finding a good reason is not always easy. Letter 99 shows one way of approaching such a request.

Making an objection
Letter 101 deals with making an objection to a local authority about a planned development and gives hints on how to put your message across in the strongest terms, to make the maximum impact.

This letter is a response to a request for financial help towards a children's hospice. The company is responding positively to the request, with both financial and practical help. The practical help in this instance will be appreciated as much as the purely financial.

Kelso Limited
16 Abbots Road, Luton, Bedford MK44 7YT
Tel: (01234) 136953 Fax: (01234) 136422
Registered in England No: 9126719 VAT No: 91523489 76

Ms J Parish
Churchill House
Saffron Close
Luton
Bedford
MK44 7YH

28 July 1999

Dear Ms Parish,

Thank you for your letter of 14 July about your plans for a Children's Hospice in Luton.

It is not normally our policy to make charitable donations but we were so moved by the plight of the children that you care for that we have decided to make an exception. I am delighted to enclose a cheque for £1,000 on behalf of everyone at Kelso Limited.

In addition, I would also like to offer more practical help with the building conversion. As one of the leading builders in Luton, we are willing to release three of our men for a week, to help you with any aspect of the building work. We have skills in bricklaying, plastering, tiling and other general structural changes and I would be pleased to discuss ways in which we may be able to make a contribution.

Yours sincerely

Tony Southgate
Director

PARKER
Glass Ltd

Unit 27 Willow Park
Christchurch, Dorset BH23 6MM
Tel: 01202 109111
Fax: 01202 109112

Reg. No: England 962578762
VAT No: 9120564

David Firth
Christchurch Business Club
19 Buttercup Gardens
Christchurch
Dorset
BH23 5MM

28 July 1999

Dear David,

Re: Presentation to the Christchurch Business Club
Thank you for your letter of 20 July, about the Christchurch
Business Club meeting on 10 October.

I confirm that I will be available to give a short presentation on how
we do business and the successful team behind our venture. I
would appreciate it, though, if you could indicate how many people
you expect to attend; how long the presentation is expected to last
and how many other presentations there will be. I would expect to
accompany my talk with a few slides. Can you also confirm if there
is a 35mm slide projector and screen available?

I would also like, if possible, to be one of the earlier speakers in the
event.

I look forward to hearing from you.

Yours sincerely

Roger Crabb
Marketing Director

If you are asked to give a presentation or talk, it pays to do as much research as you can. If you are not clear about the type of people attending and what their interests are, find out, so your talk can be tailored to their needs. You will also need to know how long the talk should be, and whether the right technical equipment is available.

If you can, always request to be one of the earlier speakers in the day: your audience will be more alert and inclined to listen then. After lunch is a bad time, as is the last slot of the day, because your audience may be itching to leave and the other speakers may have over-run on their time, leaving you with less time than you have prepared for, to get your message across.

A letter declining to give a donation is not easy to write. But not replying at all is discourteous and bad for your public relations. Remember, the person writing to you may also be a customer. The problem with declining a donation is that it is easy to appear mean-minded and uncharitable. This letter provides a good reason that will be understood by the charity.

Tyler & Piper Associates

76 Whites Lane, Stevenage, Herts SG1 8JP England
Tel: (01438) 186465 Fax: (01438) 164323

Mr Paul Middleton
H.D.S.C.F
14 Franklin Gardens
Mildenhall
Suffolk
IP28 7JU

3 February 1999

Dear Mr Middleton,

Thank you for your letter about your extremely worthy cause, offering holidays to disabled children in Suffolk.

As a small company employing only 20 people we have only limited funds available for charitable donations each year. As such, we have to set down strict criteria for the causes to which we will donate. One of the prime considerations is the area which the cause will benefit. I understand that the holidays are for children in the Suffolk area and I regret that this is outside the region in which we have decided to concentrate our charitable work and we must, therefore, regretfully decline your invitation.

I am sorry for the disappointment this will undoubtedly cause but I do hope you understand our reasons. We do, however, hope your venture succeeds and I would like to take this opportunity to wish you every success.

Yours sincerely

S R Piper

Partners: DA Tyler BA & SR Piper MA

PARKER

Glass Ltd

Unit 27 Willow Park
Christchurch, Dorset BH23 6MM
Tel: 01202 109111
Fax: 01202 109112

Reg. No: England 962578762
VAT No: 9120564

David Firth
Christchurch Business Club
19 Buttercup Gardens
Christchurch
Dorset
BH23 5MM

28 May 1999

Dear David,

Thank you very much for your invitation to speak at your business club meeting on 10 June.

Unfortunately, I shall be away on holiday when your meeting is planned and unavailable to speak personally. However, my colleague and fellow director, David Harvey (who knows our business intimately), would be willing to speak in my place.

May I suggest you call him on 01202 109111, to discuss the arrangements?

Yours sincerely

Roger Crabb
Marketing Director

If you are unable to attend a function that offers a good public-relations opportunity, try to nominate someone else to take your place. You won't be letting the organiser down or missing out on the chance to tell people about your business.

Objections to an authority like this must be supported by strong factual reasons why your objection is justified, if you are to have any sway with the deciding authority. 'Because we don't like it' will not be sufficient.

Note how the company adds weight to the objection, by making it seem as if Shortly's already has insufficient car-parking space which is being abused, as the company has "...already had to make several representations...".

The strongest argument is saved until the end: pointing out that the application does not conform to the local regulations. These arguments give credibility to the strength of the opening phrase of the final paragraph: "We object in the strongest terms...".

Hart & Tucker Ltd

19 Green Street, Maidstone, Kent ME41 1TJ
Telephone: (01622) 109109
Facsimile: (01622) 108106
Reg. No: England 96223978 VAT No: 91210674

Kent County Council
Council Chambers
Maidstone
Kent
ME41 3OD

For the attention of the Planning Officer:

24 May 1999

Dear Sirs,

Re: Planning application for Shortly's Building in Green Street
We are in receipt of the application for a new factory building for Shortly Ltd, on Green Street.

On inspecting the plans, we are extremely concerned to find that insufficient provision appears to have been made for the additional car parking that will be necessary for the increase in staff, deliveries and visitors that the new building will generate. Our concern is amplified by the fact that, at present, we operate a shared car park with Shortly's and have already had to make several representations to them for using spaces which are allocated to us.

We understand from the announcements in the press that the building is required because they are relocating their Witchbury site to the Green Street operation. We understand that there will be no job losses resulting from this relocation and the same number of staff will be working in Green St as were employed in Witchbury. I understand the Witchbury operation had provision for over 100 car parking spaces, yet the additional number allowed for here is only 60 spaces. We also understand that the local regulations state that there should be at least one car parking space for each 50 square metres of office space. With just over 5000 square metres of new office space there should be a minimum of 100 extra spaces provided for.

We object in the strongest terms to the application as it stands and would ask you to reconsider the plan in the light of these points, which clearly do not conform to current local planning requirements.

Yours sincerely

Tony Kidd
Director

301 ways to start your letter

As discussed ... requested ... agreed ...

As discussed, will you please send ...
As discussed, I enclose samples of ...
As discussed, I am very sorry for the delay in sending you ...
As requested, I enclose ...
As we agreed this morning, I would like to confirm our mutual decision ...
At our last meeting, it was agreed that ...

As you are aware ...

As I am sure you are aware, ...
As I have previously explained to you, ...
As you are aware, under our holiday policy, the company reserves the right ...
As you are no doubt aware, there are certain confidential and personal files ...
As you are no doubt aware, the recent events in ...
As you know, we deal with a number of different suppliers ...
As you know, we have been working ...

Congratulations ...

Congratulations.
Congratulations on winning ...
Firstly, Mary, I would like to say how delighted I am for you at your news ...
Many congratulations on the birth of your son.
May I be the first to offer you our congratulations on ...
I was delighted to hear you have won ...
I would like to offer you my personal congratulations ...

I am sorry ...

Firstly, apologies for the delay in replying to your fax, which was caused by ...
First of all, my sincere apologies for not responding to your enquiries ...
Firstly, I would like to say how sorry we are that you have had to wait so long ...

I am sorry if this messes you around but our client has just notified us that ...
I am sorry that you feel that you have not received the level of service expected.
I am sorry that you feel the price of ...
I am sorry to hear that you are unable to trace ...
I am sorry to learn of your recent bereavement.
I am very sorry that you were left waiting ...
I am very sorry to hear that you are still not making a good enough recovery ...
I am very sorry.
What can I say? Sorry.
Oops! We've made a real clanger.
We were all very saddened to learn about the sudden death of your wife ...
We were deeply shocked by John's untimely death ...
We were shocked and saddened to hear of Howard Green's fatal accident.
I was very sorry to hear your sad news.
I write as one of Howard's new customers to say how very, very sad we were ...

Following ...

Following our conversation this morning, I am delighted to confirm our offer ...
Following our telephone conversation ...
Following the recent accident involving ...
Following the staff meeting this morning, I am writing to confirm that ...
Following your claim for ...

Further to ...

Further to our recent discussion, I have pleasure in enclosing ...
Further to our recent telephone conversation, I have pleasure in enclosing ...
Further to our telephone conversation, I am writing to introduce you to our ...
Further to your fax this morning: at the moment I am feeling very let down by your ...
Further to your recent conversation with ...
Further to your request for ...

I ...

I note from my diary that you have an appointment to see me on ...
I promised to let you have details of ...
I realise that I should not have ...
I recently saw details of your company's range of ...
I telephoned your office last week for a revised quotation ...
I think it was very useful to talk through your performance over the last six months ...
I don't dispute that other customers have accepted ...
I wrote to you on the 16th September chasing the above order for ...

I am surprised ... disappointed ...

Bob, you personally gave me your word and I trusted you to pay promptly ...
I am surprised to have had no response to my fax dated ...
I am surprised to have received no reply to our previous letter ...
I am afraid that our Financial Director has put these orders on hold ...
I am at a loss to understand why you have not paid us the monies which you owe.
I am extremely disappointed that I find myself having to write to you yet again.
I am now getting very concerned that we have heard nothing from you ...
I am very disappointed that you have not remitted the sum of ...
I am very disappointed with you.
I hoped that I would not have to write to you about ...
I have now sent you a number of fax messages and am disappointed ...
We regret to note that you have failed to respond to our previous reminders ...

I am pleased ...

I am pleased to confirm your appointment as agent for ...
I am pleased to inform you that the company agrees to ...
I am pleased to quote you ex-works prices for the items, as requested.
I am delighted to confirm that you are this year's winner of ...
I am delighted to report that we have had an excellent year ...
I am delighted to say that our sales are ahead of expectations ...
It was a pleasure to meet you and Richard in February ...
It was a pleasure to meet you yesterday, ...
It was great to meet you and your team last week.

I have received ...

I have received a consignment of ...
I have received in the post this morning your invoice no. ...
I have received your catalogue of ...
I am in receipt of your fax of 10 February.
I am in receipt of your letter of 30 June, asking for a reference for ...
I received a copy of your autumn catalogue, giving details of ...
I received, this morning, your invoice no. ...
Yesterday, we received ...
We received your delivery of ...
We today received from you ...
We have received an application from ...

I am writing ...

I am writing concerning your request for a refund ...
I am writing on a matter that is causing ...
I am writing to advise you of a change in our terms and conditions ...
I am writing to clarify the position about the ...

I am writing to confirm our telephone conversation, regarding ...
I am writing to express my growing dissatisfaction of the service we are receiving ...
I am writing to let you know that we have decided not to renew your contract ...
I am writing to thank you for recommending me to ...
I am writing to you because I want you to know of our experience ...
I am responding to the idea that you put forward ...

I confirm ...

I confirm our faxed quotation for ...
I confirm our quote of ...
I confirm that, as of today, we are amending your terms of contract ...
I confirm the points we discussed at our meeting on ...
Just a note to confirm our conversation today ...
Just a quick note to confirm the deal agreed ...
I would just like to confirm that we have considered your request to ...
I write to confirm our order for ...
Confirming my telephone call and your return fax, ...
This is to confirm our meeting at your offices at 10.30am tomorrow, 25 January.
This is to confirm the details and the key terms of the offer we have accepted ...

I enclose ...

I enclose, herewith, a draft copy of ...
I enclose our purchase order for ...
Please find enclosed our cheque to the value of ...
Please find enclosed our statement as at 31 July for £2903.86.

It is ...

It is not often I receive such an abusive letter. In spite of your rude tone ...
It is with a tinge of sadness that I have to announce ...
It is with regret that I tender my resignation as ...
It has come to my attention that you ...
It was useful to review your progress to date ...

I have ...

I have been advised by ...
I have been given your name by ...
I have checked my records and realise that ...
I have considered your letter of 21st January and your assertion that ...
I have just been reviewing ...
I have just come across a product that is so good ...
I have just received your ...
I have just returned from a visit to ...
I have now reviewed your proposal to ...

I hope ...

I hope the last order we supplied to you was satisfactory and met your expectations.
I hope you and Joshua are well and that you are not having too many sleepless nights.

I refer to ...

I refer to our order dated ...
I refer to our order for ...
I refer to our telephone conversation this morning.
I refer to your letter of 11 February.
I refer to your letter of 23rd April 1999 about a consignment of ...

I trust ...

I trust that you enjoyed your break.
I trust that you received our consignment ...
I trust that you have received my previous correspondence.

I understand ...

I understand from my colleague, ...
I understand from our Mr Davies that you are considering moving ...
I understand that, to obtain the price that is right for us, you have asked us to take ...
I understand that you are concerned about the amount of time you have been given ...
We understand that ...

I was appalled ... astonished ... concerned ...

I was appalled to learn that our consignment had not arrived on time with you.
I was astonished when I telephoned your accounts department this morning ...
I was extremely concerned to hear that you have not received ...
I was most disturbed to receive your letter of 20 April, informing me of ...
I was very disturbed to receive your letter, concerning ...
I was given your verbal assurances on Tuesday that you would have no problem ...

I would like to ...

I would like to correct a factual error in your ...
I would like to place a firm order for ...
I would like to remind you of our agreement ...
I would like to tackle a problem that we have come across, ...

Many thanks for ...

Many thanks for agreeing to act as our ...
Many thanks for the cheque for £...., received this morning.
Many thanks for the letters received from both John and yourself, concerning ...

Many thanks for your enquiry for ...
Many thanks for your excellent talk, which ...
Many thanks for your latest offerings.
Many thanks for your letter, asking if we are prepared to offer ...
Many thanks for your letter of 13th January.
Many thanks for your order, received today.

Please ...

Please arrange for the consignment of ...
Please let me have a price on Tuesday 4 April for ...
Please find enclosed our cheque to the value of ...
Please find enclosed our statement as at 31 July for £2903.86.
Please find attached our order for ...
Please find our cheque to the value of £1123.60 to cover our order ...
Please supply a quotation for the following: ....
Please supply and deliver as follows: ...

Thanks for ...

Thanks for coming in to see me last week.
Thanks for coming to put the ...
Thanks for looking into the possibility of arranging ...
Thanks for sending through the latest price changes.
Thanks for your delivery of ...
Thanks for your quotation for ...
Thanks for your fax of 9th May. Sorry that I have sat on it for so long ...

Thank you ....

I felt I had to write to you to say how delighted I have been with ...
Just a note to say thank you for the cheque.
Just a quick note to thank you very much for your time the other day ...
Thank you for allowing me time to assess the above product.
Thank you for applying for a Credit Account with us.
Thank you for asking if we would be interested in buying ...
Thank you for attending the interview last week for the post of ...
Thank you for being so frank and open about the difficulties that you have ...
Thank you for bringing the lower than expected performance to my attention.
Thank you for buying ...
Thank you for coming to see me last ...
Thank you for contacting me about ...
Thank you for letting me know about ...
Thank you for returning the ...
Thank you for sending ... ...
Thank you for taking the trouble to clarify the situation for me.

Thank you for the business which you have brought to us.
Thank you for the courtesy extended to me during my visit to ...
Thank you for your application for a credit account.
Thank you very much indeed for your extremely pleasant letter ...
Thank you very much for arranging a most enjoyable day for me.

Thank you for your ...

Thank you for your application for the post of ...
Thank you for your cheque for £1500 in part settlement of your account.
Thank you for your comments on our proposed discount.
Thank you for your completed application form for the position of ...
Thank you for your enquiry about the price of ...
Thank you for your fax, which I received this morning, asking if ...
Thank you for your fax, regarding payment for your orders.
Thank you for your invoice no. ...
Thank you for your kind invitation to ...
Thank you for your latest delivery, received today
Thank you for your letter dated 17th February, addressed to our Managing Director, which has been brought to my attention.
Thank you for your letter dated 9th September, addressed to our Managing Director, who has passed this to me for my attention.
Thank you for your letter expressing concern about the service you are receiving ...
Thank you for your letter of 11th September and for the samples ...
Thank you for your letter of 12 June, concerning the carriage charge on our invoice.
Thank you for your letter of 12 June, outlining the terms ...
Thank you for your letter of 15 July, notifying us that ...
Thank you for your letter of 20 June, regarding ...
Thank you for your letter of 21 May, advising us ...
Thank you for your letter of 24 June, applying for the post of ...
Thank you for your letter of 26 January, asking about the terms for ...
Thank you for your letter of 3 June, enquiring if we have any vacancies for ...
Thank you for your letter of 30 April in response to our order ...
Thank you for your letter of 3rd December and for your kind comments.
Thank you for your letter of 7th March, which reached me today.
Thank you for your letter of the 5th July, expressing concern over ...
Thank you for your letter, querying the price of ...
Thank you for your order against our quotation no. ...
Thank you for your payment of £..., which, I note, was credited to our account ...
Thank you for your prices, received this morning.
Thank you for your proposed price ...
Thank you for your recent enquiry.
Thank you for your recent faxes. I apologise for the delay in replying.
Thank you for your recent order for the enclosed ...
Thank you for your recent order. I am afraid that we have temporarily sold out of ...

119

Thank you for your recent telephone call, regarding ...
Thank you for your request for a reference for ...
Thank you for your suggestion that we ...
Thank you for your telephone call today.
Thank you for your time on Tuesday, concerning ...
Thank you very much for your letter about ...

We...

We are a small company, specialising in ...
We are currently seeking to be registered ...
We are in receipt of your cheque for ...
We are intending to trade with ...
We are interested in ...
We are pleased to announce the appointment of ...
We are reorganising the administration of our accounts department ...
We have an outstanding debt of ...
We have been notified by ...
We have considered your request to operate an agency ...
We have decided to change the holiday policy of the company.
We have just learned about the death of ...
We have just secured an unexpectedly large order ...
We have noticed some abuses of the telephone for private calls ...
We have recently received the enclosed Statement from you.
We have reviewed the price changes to our products for the next 12 months.
We have supplied you with items on four separate occasions to the value of ...
We met at the Multimedia 99 show (on the Wednesday) and you showed me ...
We no longer need ...
We note that you have failed to respond to our previous demands to settle ...
We wish to obtain ...
We would like to carry out some amendments to ...

With reference to ...

With reference to our recent telephone conversation, ...
With reference to our telephone conversation, I have pleasure in introducing ...
With reference to the above, we have received ...
With regard to the above, we enclose ...
Re: your fax to our accounts manager of ...
Re: your recommendation of ...

You ...

You have been issued with ...
You have been specially selected to receive one of our star prizes ...
You have received two written warnings about ...

You may have heard rumours circulating ...
You supplied us with a new ...

Your ...

Your account has been passed to me for attention ...
Your account with us is now SERIOUSLY OVERDUE.
Your company has opened a credit account with us.
Your customer ... has applied to us for a credit account ...
Your subscription to ... will be expiring within the next three months.

More notes to start on ...

A week ago, you arranged for ...
According to my records, you still owe ...
As a company committed to providing a quality service, ...
As you are a valued customer, we want every pound you spend with us to save you money.
Having arrived back safely ...
Here is our ...
In April this year, you ordered ...
In case you failed to receive the details we sent last month of our fabulous ...
In conversation with your colleague, Mary, yesterday, it emerged that ...
In response to your telephone enquiry this morning, I am writing to announce that ...
Just a quick note to let you know that ...
On 30 September, we placed an order for ...
On 6 August, we received from you a consignment of ...
On a recent visit to your company, I left our company brochure for your attention ...
Our agreement of 20 January stipulates that you undertake to supply us with ...
Payment for this order was due in ...
The response to our advertisement for an Office Manager has exceeded ...
Since we have acquired ...
Something very peculiar appears to have been happening with ...
Until now, it has been a requirement of the company that everyone ...
With the departure of ...

201 nice turns of phrase

This appendix selects over 200 of the best phrases for you to choose from. It concentrates on phrases with mood and emotion so, whether you are having to write a letter of condolence, persuade someone to your way of thinking or bring a supplier up sharply, you are certain to find the right phrase to fit the moment.

Stern phrases

I trust our purchase order instructions will be rigidly adhered to in future.

As they have not been received by the due date, we are exercising our right under the agreement to cancel the order forthwith.

I was surprised to see a carriage charge included for ...

No mention was made of this charge ...

Our purchase order referred expressly to the fact that delivery was to be included in the price ...

You may recall that when I placed the order, you granted us a special discount ...

... it should be little more than an extension of what your current practices are ...

We expect our suppliers to give us the service that we demand ...

It will certainly make us think twice about using you in the future ...

Unless you can agree to do our printing profitably within the price agreed, we will probably have to agree to part company.

I expect a full refund by return.

We shall have no option but to seek an alternative supplier.

I am therefore bound to advise you that ...

Please give it your most urgent attention.

It is time this matter was brought to a close.

... we shall not hesitate in disallowing the commission payment ...

... it is naturally disconcerting ...

It is also particularly disappointing ...

You have not had the authority ...

I was led to believe that this was included in your quotation
... your failure to notify us ...
Your conduct in this matter has been extremely disappointing ...
I was very disturbed ...
... we have already had to make several representations ...
We object in the strongest terms ...
I hope this makes our position clear ...
We expect you to accomplish it within the agreed deadline and budget.
We must have a solution if you are to retain our custom.
I regard this behaviour as totally unprofessional.
I am not satisfied that the goods are of merchantable quality.
Since the goods are not fit for the purpose intended ...
I must stress that, in placing this order with you, ...
... it was absolutely conditional on your ability to meet our deadline.
... for which we shall seek compensation.
I was astounded to find that ...
... we shall be seeking recompense for any losses that we incur.
... the occasion was a shambolic disaster from start to finish.
I strongly sense that you are taking us for granted ...
... the entire job is simply unacceptable...
I am particularly irritated that, once again, you are blaming ...
I am hoping that you will take these issues more seriously than your colleagues appear
   to ...

Contractual phrases

Under the terms of our agreement ...
... I trust that you will abide by the terms of our agreement.
I would like to draw your attention to the agreement...
Our agreement expressly forbids you ...
... in full and final settlement ...
... it was a condition of our contract ...
As you have not kept to the terms of your contract ...
... failure to comply with our terms ...
... we shall have no option but to terminate ...
... we are exercising our right not to pay ...
... we undertake to rectify ...
... we have made good the defect ...
... we have honoured our contract to you ...
... we shall have no option but to terminate ...

Letting someone down lightly

At the moment, it does not fit in comfortably with our plans for the immediate future ...

124

I am afraid I must say "Thanks, but no thanks".
Our decision was arrived at after a great deal of discussion and thought.
It was not an easy decision to make ...
While I believe that your experience is right for us, ...
I am confident that you would be able to secure a good number of orders for our business but ...
... it would not be fair to either of us ...

Phrases that trigger people's emotional responses

You will understand that, as a business, we put a high premium on reliability.
I am feeling very let down by your company ...
... don't have a moral leg to stand upon ...
... really should know better ...
It was not we who caused this problem ...

Phrases that charm customers

... as a special favour ...
... enclosed is the guarantee which sets out our promises and your rights ...
We look forward to a long and happy association with your business.
Should we fall short of your high expectations in any matter ...
... please contact me personally.
... and trust that this helps in compensating you for your dissatisfaction.
We are, of course, concerned to offer you the best possible service ...
... as you are a highly valued customer ...
Anticipating that this arrangement will be acceptable to you, I have pleasure in enclosing ...
... you have been specially chosen ...
... we are asking a select group of our customers ...
... you will avoid immeasurable hassle ...

Making a gentle request

... we will have to ask you ...
... I do not consider it unreasonable to ask you to ...
I don't want to put you to any trouble, but it would be enormously helpful ...
I appreciate this is a busy time for you, but I wonder if ...
It therefore does not seem unreasonable to request ...

Phrases that aim to reassure

I confirm that we are happy to stand by our original quotation.
I assure you it is perfectly normal and will not impede its function.
... it does not fulfil the high standard that we demand and you, as a customer, expect.
... would not dream of stepping beyond the powers ...

I am appalled at how you have been treated ...
I was most disturbed to receive your letter ...
... the intention is not to squeeze a quart out of a pint pot.
... before you come running to us crying 'foul' ...
I know how frustrating it is to be left high and dry ...
I trust everything is in order ...

Making sincere apologies

If I could perhaps explain the circumstances that occurred, not as an excuse, but so you can see the exceptional and unexpected difficulties that we faced.
I am deeply sorry that we have let you and your client down ...
This unfortunate event has highlighted a gap in our procedures.
I am extremely sorry this has occurred ...
This is a very rare occurrence (it happens about once a year) ...
Please accept our unreserved apologies.
I have made enquiries and have discovered that in this instance one of our internal procedural systems failed.
I do hope that this will go some way to restoring your faith in us.
It seems you have been plagued by gremlins on this occasion.
I have pushed you to the front of the waiting list ...
We are all real people in this company, who try very hard indeed to give a fast and efficient service.
I am sorry that you feel that you have not received the level of service expected.
I am confident that you should not experience the same level of disruption now.
I am sorry for any inconvenience caused.
I apologise for this oversight ...

Refusing and rejecting

I regret that we are unable to assist you further in this matter.
For this reason, I regret we must decline your kind invitation ...
I am sorry that we cannot be more helpful on this occasion.
Although, as is clear, I do not agree with much of your letter ...
... I very much regret that we must insist ...
While we do not like to impose unnecessary restrictions ...
I regret that we have decided not to take your application further on this occasion.
I have to be completely honest and say that there is no way we can pay ...
... I wish to deny in the strongest terms possible ...
... we refute your claim.
... I cannot think of any circumstance in which I would dream of agreeing ...
I do not accept your assertions ...

Persuasive phrases

... the charge reflects a contribution only towards the final cost ...
... we do everything we can to keep the charges as competitive as possible ...
... all our suppliers accept it, without exception ...
... we shall have no option but to seek an alternative supplier.
... I guarantee that you will experience the best ...
... we have striven to keep the price increases to an absolute minimum ...
... we see this as a modest contribution towards our continued mutual success ...
... it would not be in our best interests ...
... we are taking on the chin the cost of inflation and the increased cost of ...

Chasing payment

We have now decided to take legal advice on this matter, with a view to the recovery of our money ...
... instructions will be issued to our solicitors to proceed against you.
... please arrange immediate settlement.
... this thorny issue of payment ...
... remit this by return ...
... in view of the one-sided nature of our correspondence ...
... the matter will be passed into other hands in seven days.
... I hope you will render this action unnecessary ...
If you have sent your remittance in the last few days, please disregard this letter.
No further reminders will be issued.
We appreciate this act of good faith ...
... despite our best efforts to obtain payment from you ...

Responding to requests for payment

The reasons for the delay are both tedious and convoluted.
Should any future invoices slip through the net ...
I am extremely embarrassed about the long delay ...

Praise, flattery and recognition

... because you are the best person for the job ...
I will respect your decision, whatever it is.
... thank you personally for all the hard work ...
Thank you once again for your major contribution ...
... the best minds are devoted to this project ...
... I am delighted to announce that you are eligible to receive ...
Congratulations on taking the initiative ...
... I am very impressed by their versatility ...
Your role in this is, of course, pivotal.
... I applaud your enthusiasm for not missing a sale ...

127

It will be a tremendous honour ...
It gives me great personal pleasure to recognise ...

Threatening to take legal action

While we have no quarrel with your business ...
... we intend to take legal action against ...
... unless she agrees to abide by the terms of our agreement ...
... we shall commence legal proceedings against her.

Warnings

I must warn you ...
... we find it inexcusable ...
... failure to do so ...
You have been given every opportunity ...
As you have chosen to ignore all the warnings ...
... we have no alternative ...
... you must not undertake ...
... you were unable to give us a satisfactory reason ...

Offering help and assistance

... we shall be only too happy to provide ...
We will do everything we can to help ...
... I shall be keeping my fingers crossed.

Motivational

... I know you will be very capable of successfully accomplishing ...
You have a great deal to contribute ...
I am confident that there will be considerable opportunities to increase your
    responsibilities.
I know you will do your utmost ...
I know you will be able to make a major contribution ...
... it is a tribute to your hard work ...
It means a great deal to me, personally, ...

Condolence

We were deeply shocked ...
... it will be very difficult for us to forget ...
We will miss him sorely.
Please accept our sincere sympathy.
We were shocked and saddened ...

Selling phrases

... will cut a swathe through the tasks ...
By far the best, ever.
... that makes the guide, for me, utterly irresistible.
... quickly and confidently ...
Do have a look at it ...
... a return that is <u>absolutely guaranteed</u>.
... you do not, absolutely not, have to buy anything from us ...
What do you have to lose?
I have just come across ...
... we felt it essential to let you know about it ...
Just complete the fax-back acceptance offer ... before everyone else does.
... outstanding value for money ...

Appealing for donations

... go a little way to help ...
... find the heart to help ...
... It's not a lot to ask ...

Keeping your options open

Your payment terms are subject to the timing of our payment runs.
However, we reserve the right to return ...

Keeping a supplier firmly *on* the hook

I accept this as a gesture of apology but not as a satisfactory recompense for the late
delivery.

Exaggerating a point slightly

It has cost us up to £400 more a month ...

Preparing the ground for bad news

I very much regret that, as from 1st May, we must increase prices of this product ...

185 ways to finish your letter

Best ...

Best regards.
Best wishes.
Best wishes and good luck.
Best wishes from myself and all at ...

I ...

I am grateful that you took the trouble to write ...
I am returning the item with this letter and expect a full refund of ...
I am sorry for any inconvenience caused.
I am sorry that we cannot be more helpful on this occasion.
I do hope that this will go some way to restoring your faith in us.
I enclose a stamped addressed envelope for your convenience when you reply.
I have pleasure in enclosing ...
I have pleasure in returning the product as required ...
I must insist that, from now on, we are given priority treatment.
I regret that we are unable to assist you further in this matter.
I therefore look forward to your immediate reassurance ...
I very much regret that we shall be unable to offer you a refund.

I hope ...

I hope that we continue to be of benefit to you in the future.
I hope they are a success for you.
I hope this arrangement is acceptable to you.
I hope this arrangement is satisfactory.
I hope this explains the position but, if you have any other queries, please do ask.
I hope this information helps you.
I hope this makes our position clear.
I hope this matter can now be closed.
I hope this plan meets with your approval.

I hope this proposal will be of interest to you.
I hope you are willing to help us in this matter.
I hope you have a very successful and prosperous New Year.
I hope you will be able to agree to this proposal.

I look forward to ...

I look forward to a long, fruitful and communicative business relationship.
I look forward to a long and prosperous association with your company.
I look forward to continuing a close relationship with your business in the future.
I look forward to hearing from you and, of course, to receiving your order.
I look forward to hearing from you at your earliest convenience.
I look forward to hearing from you shortly.
I look forward to hearing from you, with regard to ...
I look forward to hearing from you.
I look forward to meeting you all again soon.
I look forward to meeting you.
I look forward to receiving confirmation of your order.
I look forward to receiving your remittances by return.
I look forward to receiving your reply.
I look forward to seeing you again shortly.
I look forward to seeing you on your next visit to the UK.
I look forward to your advice on this matter.
I look forward to your further enquiries.
I look forward to your immediate response.

I trust ...

I trust that further action will now be taken and look forward to your response.
I trust that you find these of interest.
I trust that you will abide by the terms of our agreement.
I trust this gives you the information that you require.
I trust this is a satisfactory summary of our conversation.
I trust this is all in order and hope that you are satisfied with the goods as supplied.
I trust this summarises our conversation satisfactorily.
I trust you will take the above into account.

I would ...

I would appreciate it if you could amend your records accordingly.
I would appreciate it if you could settle the account by the end of this month.
I would be grateful if one of your representatives could telephone me ...
I would be grateful if you could arrange for ....
I would be grateful if you could confirm safe receipt.
I would like to take this opportunity to wish you every success in your future.

If ...

If anyone has any queries about this new policy, please come and see me at any time.
If I can be of any further assistance to you, please do not hesitate to contact me.
If not, please arrange immediate settlement.
If there is anything we can do, please let us know.
If this is of interest, let me know.

If you ...

If you are interested in any of these, do give me a call.
If you are still unable to locate the item, please let me know.
If you do not receive the items by next Tuesday, please let me know.
If you have any further queries on this matter, please contact me again.
If you have any further questions, please do not hesitate to contact me.
If you have any more queries, please do not hesitate to contact me.
If you have any queries, please give me a call.
If you have any queries, please contact me on ...
If you have any questions, or need any further information, please give me a call.
If you have sent your remittance in the last few days, please disregard this letter.
If you need further information, please do not hesitate to contact us.
If you require any further information, please do not hesitate to ask.
If you would like further information, please ring us on ...

In the meantime ...

In the meantime, please could you arrange for ...
In the meantime, I shall ensure that ...
In the meantime, if you have any queries, please give me a ring.

It ...

It is essential that these instructions are adhered to, strictly.
It is time this matter was brought to a close.
It would be appreciated if you could let me know, by return.

Kind ...

Kind regards
Kindest regards.

Let me know ...

Let me know if this is of interest to you.
Let me know if you find out any details and, once again, many thanks for your help.
Let me know what you decide. I will respect your decision, whichever way it goes.
Let me know your thoughts.

Many thanks for ...

Many thanks for your co-operation.
Many thanks for your help.
Many thanks for your prompt and courteous attention to this matter.
Many thanks for your time and effort on our behalf.

Once again, ...

Once again, please accept our sincerest apologies.
Once again, please accept our apologies.
Once again, my sincere apologies.
Once again, thank you very much indeed for taking the trouble to write to me.

Please accept ...

Please accept my apologies for this delay.
Please accept our most sincere condolences and deepest sympathy, from all at ...
Please accept our sincere apologies for the distress caused.
Please accept our sincere apologies for this slight deterioration in service.
Please accept our sincere sympathy for your loss.
Please accept our unreserved apologies.

Please ...

Please advise me of ...
Please call me back urgently, so we can discuss this.
Please cancel ...
Please come back to me if it does not solve the problem.
Please confirm whether this time is convenient for you.
Please arrange for the balance to be supplied as soon as possible.
Please give this matter your most urgent attention.
Please let me know if anything goes wrong again.
Please do not hesitate to call me, should there be any issue that you want to discuss.
Please do not hesitate to contact us, should you need any further information.
Please do not hesitate to get in contact, if we can be of further assistance.
Please find enclosed a copy of our current price list, as requested.
Please give me a call if you would like to set up a meeting.
Please give me a ring if anything is unclear.
Please let me know if this arrangement is of interest.
Please let me know if you think this outline plan is suitable.
Please let me know when these samples will be sent.
Please, please, please supply us with the missing items ASAP.
Please telephone me on receipt of this letter, to let me know ...
Please transfer the remaining balance to account no. ...
Please try to answer these queries quickly, to enable us to ...

Should you ...

Should you be uncertain about any aspect of it, please do not hesitate to give us a call.
Should you have any urgent enquiries, please do not hesitate to contact me personally.
Should you require any further information, please do not hesitate to contact us.

Sorry ...

Sorry for any inconvenience caused by this matter.
Sorry for any trouble caused.

Thank you ...

Thank you again for your assistance, and all good wishes for a successful ...
Thank you for the interest you have shown in our Company.
Thank you for your assistance in this matter.
Thank you for your attention to this matter.
Thank you for your co-operation with this policy.
Thank you for your co-operation in this matter.
Thank you for your help with this matter.
Thank you for your interest in our range of products.
Thank you for your interest.
Thank you for your kind attention.
Thank you for your time and efforts on our behalf.
Thank you in advance for your co-operation.
Thank you, once again, for your kindness.
Thank you once again.
Thank you very much indeed for taking the trouble to write to reassure me.
Thanking you in advance.
Thanking you in anticipation of your assistance in this matter.

We hope ...

We hope never to hear from you again.
We hope you find the package of value and look forward to your future custom.

We look forward ...

We look forward to a long and happy association with your business.
We look forward to hearing from you.
We look forward to helping you save money throughout the coming year.
We look forward to receiving your payment.
We look forward to seeing you then.
We look forward to welcoming you as a customer.
We look forward to your valued, continued support.
We look forward to receiving your cheque by return.

We ...

We regret, therefore, that we must decline your kind offer.
We shall keep you informed, as and when developments occur.
We thank you for this order and look forward to your further enquiries.
We very much appreciate your help in this matter.
We would appreciate your quotation by fax and at the latest by Thursday 12 June.

With ...

With kind regards.
With very best wishes,

Would you ...

Would you kindly acknowledge receipt of this letter and confirm ...
Would you kindly arrange for someone to come and ...
Would you please confirm that ...

Your ...

Your immediate response (and payment) would be appreciated.
Your order will be dispatched as soon as we receive your remittance.

More notes to end on ...

A quick reply would be much appreciated.
Any future orders will have to be paid for in advance.
As stated, we will be having no further dealings with your company.
Do let me know what you decide and I shall be keeping my fingers crossed.
Finally, I enclose the form duly completed and signed.
Give me a call to let me know when you are coming.
Hope to speak to you soon.
Just tick the box on the enclosed reply-paid envelope and send it back to us.
May we take this opportunity of thanking you for your valued support during ...
Regards.
The agenda for this meeting is attached.
This does not help to foster confidence in our business together.
To find out how we can help you, call me now on ...
Whatever the cause of the delay may be, we must have a solution ...

INDEX

Free Special Report

(published price £14.95)

Which one would you like?

- ☐ Dirty Negotiating Tactics and their Solutions
- ☐ Organise Yourself to be Lazy
- ☐ Clear Your Desk Once and For All
- ☐ How to Bankrupt a Rogue Company
- ☐ The Two Minute Presentation Planner
- ☐ Achieving ISO9000 - How much will it cost?
- ☐ Finding and Bidding for Bargain Properties at Auction

We would like to send you the Free Special Report of your choice.

Why?

Because we would like to add your name to our Business Enquirers Group – a selection of business people who receive regular information from us. We will offer you the best and most practical business books published, newsletters, a book review service and also offers from other companies with products and services that may interest you.

To order your free report and join the Business Enquirers Group, simply phone fax or write, give us your name, job title, address, phone, fax and e-mail numbers (if available) and quote MM02. And don't forget to tell us which report you want!

☎ 01353 665544

Ask for your free report by title and remember to quote our reference MM02

Fax 01353 667666

Photocopy this page, complete this box and fax it through to us

Name _____	Job title _____
Company _____	
Address _____	
_____ Post code _____	
Phone _____ Fax _____ e-mail _____	

Post

Wyvern Business Library MM02, FREEPOST CB511, Ely, Cambs CB7 4BR

Photocopy this page, fill in the box above (or staple your business card to it) and send it to us (no stamp required).